Heads up

Spoken English for business — B1

Mark Tulip with *Louise Green and Richard Nicholas*

AF092846

 Access all the accompanying digital components for this book on **allango**, the DELTA Publishing language learning platform:

 Scan the QR code or go directly to **www.allango.co.uk** | Search for the title or the ISBN and click on the cover image | Access content, use now or save for later

 When you see this symbol, accompanying digital content is available.

DELTA Publishing

Author Mark Tulip with Louise Green and Richard Nicholas

Editor Catriona Watson-Brown
Layout and typesetting Ken Vail Graphic Design, Ltd.
Cover picture Shutterstock (Rawpixel.com), New York
Cover Andreas Drabarek

Information and additional products/material for this series can be found here:
www.deltapublishing.co.uk/heads-up

1st edition 1 ⁵ ⁴ ³ | 2026 25 24
The last figure shown denotes the year of impression.

DELTA Publishing, an imprint of the Ernst Klett Sprachen GmbH
© Ernst Klett Sprachen GmbH, Rotebühlstraße 77, 70178 Stuttgart, 2019

All rights reserved. The use of the contents for text and data mining is expressly reserved and therefore prohibited.
www.deltapublishing.co.uk
www.klett-sprachen.de/delta

No part of this publication may be reproduced, stored in a retrieval system, or transmitted, in any form or by any means, electronic, mechanical, photocopying, recording, or otherwise, without prior written permission from the publisher.

Printing and binding Elanders GmbH, Waiblingen

ISBN 978-3-12-501316-2

Contents

My job

1	What do you do?	4
2	My contacts	6
3	My phone calls	8
4	My diary	10
5	Socialising 1: Welcoming, introducing, greeting and saying goodbye	12
6	Soft skills	14
7	Presentations 1: Structuring and starting	16
8	Presentations 2: Moving forward and ending	18
9	Managing my time	20
10	My procedures	22
11	Stress	24
12	Socialising 2: Asking about and ordering food, making conversation	26
13	Problem-solving	28
14	Travel	30
15	My career	32

My business

16	My company	34
17	Our products and services	36
18	Our company structure	38
19	Connecting online	40
20	Meetings 1: Giving opinions, agreeing and disagreeing	42
21	Figures	44
22	Trends	46
23	Socialising 3: Entertaining at home	48
24	The marketing mix	50
25	Selling	52
26	Know your customer	54
27	Our business online	56
28	Meetings 2: Making your point and checking understanding	58
29	Production	60
30	Orders and delivery	62
31	Socialising 4: Speaking and responding in social situations	64
32	Success and failure	66
33	Meetings 3: Managing meetings	68

The bigger picture

34	Our competitors	70
35	Our market	72
36	New communications	74
37	Import–export	76
38	Socialising 5: Talking about behaviour when doing business internationally	78
39	The economy	80
40	International business quiz	82
	Activity files	84
	Audio scripts	89
	Answer key	97
	Teachers' feedback sheet	103

01 What do you do?

Describe your work and responsibilities

1 Match the job titles (1–6) with the photos (a–f) above.

1 accountant
2 customer service operator
3 factory manager
4 salesperson
5 web developer
6 computer engineer

2 Who says what? Match these sentences (A–F) with the job titles in Exercise 1.

A I deal with customers' questions and complaints.

B I have to prepare financial reports.

C The main purpose of my job is to sell goods and services.

D I look after the company's website.

E I make and repair computers.

F I'm in charge of production.

3 What's your job title?

4 Finish this sentence.

The main purpose of my job is to …

What do you do? 01

Listening

5 ▶1 **You're going to hear a man talk about his job in a food company. Listen and complete this job description form.**

Job description	
Name of organisation:	Jonson Foods Limited
Job title:	1 _____
Department:	Quality Control
Based in:	2 _____
Full-time or part-time:	3 _____
Reports to (position):	Quality Control Manager
Main purpose of job:	Make sure 4 _____ and 5 _____ meet company standards
Other responsibilities:	6 _____

6 Check your answers to Exercise 5 with a partner.

Example:
A: Who does he work for?
B: He works for Jonson Foods Limited.

Pronunciation Intonation in *wh-* questions

Wh- questions usually go down towards the end.

Who do you work for?

Which department do you work in?

▶2 **Listen and practise saying the nine questions that you hear.**

Get ready

7 Make questions from these words.
1. Who | you work for?
2. What | job title?
3. What | the main purpose of your job?
4. What other responsibilities | you have?
5. Where | you based?
6. Which department | work in?
7. work full-time or part-time?
8. temporary or permanent position?
9. Who | you report to?
10. like your job? Why?
11. What | do before this job?
12. What | like to do in the future?

Key language
for describing your job

I work for …
I'm a(n) …
I'm based in …
I work in the … department.
I report to …
The main purpose of my job is to …
I deal with / look after …
I also have to …
I manage …
I'm in charge of …

TASK

8 Work with a partner. Use your questions from Exercise 7 to ask each other about your jobs. Use the Key language to help you.

Alternative task for pre-work students online

02 My contacts

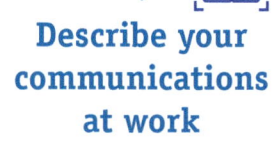

Describe your communications at work

1 Look at the means of communication in the box below. Which would you use to …
   1 tell somebody you're going to be late for a meeting?
   2 send somebody a financial report?
   3 speak to a colleague in Australia?
   4 tell five people that there's going to be a meeting next Friday?
   5 tell your customers about a special offer?
   6 fire somebody?

   e-mail   face to face   mobile phone   Skype
   social media   text/WhatsApp message

2 How has communication changed at home and at work in the last 20 years?

Listening

3 ▶3 You're going to hear Alice Peet, an assistant art director from Realgame plc, talking about the contacts she has inside and outside her organisation. Listen and tick (✓) the contacts you hear on this communications map.

internal contacts   Alice Peet   **external contacts**

- managers
- colleagues
- project workers
- other department personnel
- unions

- customers/clients
- suppliers
- other organisations
- users
- government authorities
- the media

4 ▶3 Listen again and decide if these statements are true (T) or false (F). Correct the false ones.
   1 Alice communicates most with her colleagues.
   2 She talks to her colleagues about prices.
   3 The Finance Manager thinks Alice spends too much.
   4 Alice sometimes argues with suppliers.
   5 She discusses her work with the media.

Pronunciation The weak form of to

Too, *two* and *to* can all be pronounced in the same way: /tuː/.
But in fast spoken English, *to* is normally pronounced /tə/.

1 ▶4 Listen to these questions and sentences and decide if the words in bold are pronounced /tuː/ or /tə/.
   1 What do you talk **to** them about?
   2 I speak **to** my boss.
   3 Who else do you talk **to**?
   4 I talk **to** the Finance Manager.
   5 We think our budget is **too** small.
   6 He doesn't want **to** give us any money.
   7 He thinks we spend **too** much.
   8 How often do you speak **to** them?

2 ▶4 Listen again and repeat.

My contacts 02

Key language for communication

- **say** something *He said it's expensive.*
- **tell** somebody something *She told me the price.*
- **tell/ask** somebody (not) to do something
  I asked him (not) to call me again.
- **talk/speak/listen** to somebody
  She spoke to me about the interview.
- **discuss** something with somebody
  I discussed the project with my boss.
- **agree/disagree/argue** with somebody about something
  The customer agreed with us about the price.

Means of communication
face to face
to call/ring/phone somebody
to text somebody
to talk online
to Skype somebody
to e-mail somebody
a tweet / to tweet
to message somebody on WhatsApp/Facebook

Get ready

5 Complete the gaps with the correct form of *say*, *tell* or *ask*. In some cases, more than one answer is possible.
1 The clients _____ her to do a job yesterday.
2 Yesterday, she _____ the meeting was at nine o'clock.
3 Sorry, what did you _____?
4 I _____ Kirsten to send the sample last week, but she didn't.
5 Can you _____ me the product number?
6 Last week, she _____ me not to use these suppliers again.

6 Choose the best word or phrase to complete each sentence.
1 Alice *discusses / talks* problems with clients.
2 I don't think it's a good idea. I don't *talk / agree*.
3 She sometimes *calls / texts* clients online.
4 Alice sometimes *argues / asks* with the Finance Manager about their budget.
5 I think we should talk *face to face / e-mail*.
6 We *talked / discussed* about the last order.

TASK

7 Complete this communications map with your contacts in your organisation.

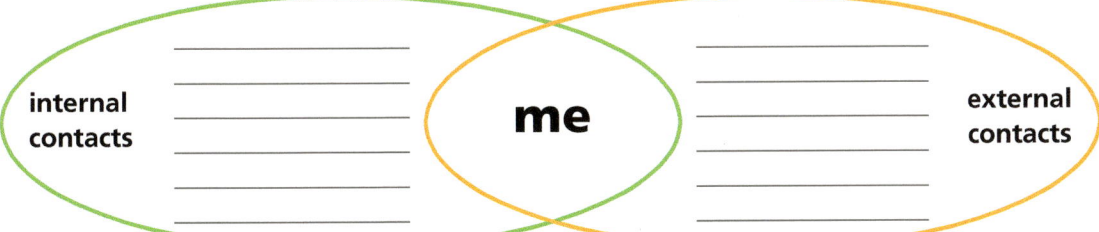

8 Work with a partner. Discuss these questions about your communications.
1 What do you talk about with each of the people in your map in Exercise 7?
2 What do your bosses tell you to do / not to do? What do you ask/tell other people to do / not to do?
3 Do you sometimes disagree with any of these people? What about?
4 Do you ever argue with them? Why?
5 Do you have any communication problems in your organisation? Why?
6 Which forms of electronic communication do you prefer? Why?
7 Do you think video links can replace face-to-face meetings? Why? / Why not?

Alternative task for pre-work students online

03 My phone calls

Make and receive telephone calls

1 Put the conversation in the correct order (1–9).

- Could you ask him to call me as soon as possible? He's got my number. It's about the meeting on Monday.
- No, that's all, thanks. Bye.
- Oh, hello. It's Pilar Rivera from Mapcorp here. Could I speak to Peter?
- Yes, but he isn't answering. Could I leave a message with you?

- Goodbye.
- Hello, Peter Jacobsen's office. **1**
- Yes, of course, I'll tell him. Was there anything else?
- I'm sorry, he's away until tomorrow. Have you tried his mobile?
- Yes, sure.

2 ▶5 Listen and check your answer.

Listening

3 ▶6 You're going to hear two phone calls. Listen and correct these messages.

Kirsten Larsen called from CTD
– problem with delivery 118-G-7
– call her on 098 163 263
– urgent!

Your wife called 16.30.
Why didn't you pick up your daughter from school? She's still there.
The trains are on strike, so your wife can't go. Turn your mobile on!

Pronunciation Backchaining

Breaking a sentence down into phrases (known as *backchaining*) can help you develop your fluency. Starting at the end is a good way to practise.

▶7 Listen and repeat the parts of the four sentences you hear.

My phone calls 03

Key language for starting calls, leaving messages and finishing calls

Call receiver

Answering the call
Good morning, Pelham Chemicals.

Asking the caller to identify him/herself
Who's calling, please?

Responding
Speaking. (*If you are the person asked for*)
Hold on / Hold the line, please. I'll connect you.
Yes, I'll pass you to him/her.

Saying somebody is not available
I'm sorry, he/she's not here at the moment.

Offering to take a message
Can I take a message?

Asking for repetition
Sorry, could you say that again, please?

Confirming information
Can I just check that? You said …
Could you send me an e-mail to confirm that, please?

Finishing the call
Was there anything else?
Thanks for calling, bye.

Caller

Starting the call
Good morning, this is Kirsten Larsen from CDT.
It's Kirsten Larsen from CDT here.

Saying who you want to speak to
Could I speak to Andrej, please?

Explaining the reason for your call
I'm calling about the meeting on Friday.

Leaving a message
Can I leave a message?
Could you ask him/her to call me back?

Leaving contact information
My mobile number is 33 2368 2368.

Finishing the call
I think that's all.
I look forward to seeing you on Friday.

Get ready

4 Work with a partner to practise this phone call. Take it in turns to be A and B.

- **A** Answer the phone.
- **B** Identify yourself and ask for someone.
- **A** Say that person is not here. Leave a message?
- **B** Leave a message.

5 Work in groups of three to practise this call.

- **A** Answer the phone.
- **B** Identify yourself and ask for C.
- **A** Call C and connect B.
- **C** Answer the phone.
- **B** Identify yourself and explain reason for call.
- **C** Answer B.
- **B** End the call.
- **C** Say goodbye.

TASK

6 Work with a partner to make and receive examples of calls from your work.
1. Make a short list of possible calls. For each call, decide:
   - who's calling who?
   - why?
2. Prepare for and make the calls with a partner. Take it in turns to make and receive the calls.

Alternative task for pre-work students online

04 My diary

Make arrangements

Make phone calls to arrange appointments

1. **A lot of people are coming to see Mr Green tomorrow. Work with a partner. Read the information and complete the chart below.**

   Mr Green is having lunch with Ms Scarlet.
   Mr Black's appointment is later than Ms Orange's.
   Mr Blue is coming earlier than Ms Scarlet.
   Ms Orange's appointment is after lunch.
   Mr Brown and Ms Pink are coming in the morning, after Mr Blue.

	10.00	11.00	13.00	15.00	16.00
Mr Blue					
Ms Scarlet			✔		
Mr Brown and Ms Pink					
Mr Black					
Ms Orange					

2. **What are you doing today? And tomorrow? Tell your partner.**

Key language for talking about arrangements	
Suggesting	**Responding**
Can we meet on Tuesday afternoon?	On Thursday, I'm visiting our head office.
What/How about Wednesday afternoon?	I'm busy all day on Friday.
What are you doing on Thursday?	I'm free on 2nd July.
Would June 28th at 11 suit you?	Sorry, I can't make it at 9.30.
Are you free at 10.30?	So/OK, see you on Monday at ten.
Shall we say 9.30?	

Listening

3. **Two people are arranging a meeting to discuss a new project. Complete the conversation with words or phrases from the Key language section.**

   Alex: Hello.
   Sue: Hello, could I speak to Alex Pond, please?
   Alex: Speaking.
   Sue: It's Sue Jafari from Camco here.
   Alex: Hello, Sue, what can I do for you?
   Sue: I'm calling about the P3 project.
   Alex: Yes, of course.
   Sue: We should really arrange a meeting here soon.
   Alex: Yes, I agree. This week's not good for me, though – I'm leaving for Warsaw tomorrow. ¹_____ next week?
   Sue: Yes, I think so. I'll just check my diary. ²_____ on Tuesday?
   Alex: No, sorry, I ³_____ on Tuesday. What about Wednesday?
   Sue: Wednesday afternoon?
   Alex: Yes, that looks OK. ⁴_____ ?
   Sue: Yes, three o'clock's fine.
   Alex: Good. ⁵_____ , see you on Wednesday at three.
   Sue: OK, bye.

4. ▶8 **Now listen and compare your answers.**

10

My diary 04

Get ready

5 **Put these time expressions in the correct column of the table below according to the preposition they need.**

> 20th March   2015   Wednesday   five o'clock   April   half past three
> the afternoon   Tuesday afternoon   June   the weekend

at	on	in
6.15 p.m.	Friday 2nd December	2016

6 **Work with a partner. You're going to meet on Monday, Tuesday or Wednesday next week to discuss the new prices for your company's products.**

Student A: Look at your diary below.

Student B: Look at your diary on page 84.

Student A
Call Student B and arrange a meeting.

	Monday	Tuesday	Wednesday
a.m.	meeting with sales team		9.00–11.00 contract talks
p.m.	14.00–15.00 interviews for Product Manager post	14.00 dentist 15.00–16.30 go to tax office	13.00 lunch with RB till 14.30 15.30–16.30 software training

TASK

7 Work with a partner and make phone calls to fix appointments with each other. Before you start, decide what the calls are about (e.g. to play a sport, to go out to a restaurant, to arrange a weekend trip, etc.).

Follow-up

8 **Work with a partner. Talk about the following.**

1 What do you say when you arrive late?
2 Are people often late for appointments in your country?
3 How do you feel when people are late for appointments or meetings?
4 Have you ever been very late for an important appointment? If so, what happened?

05 Socialising 1

Welcome visitors, introduce and greet people, say goodbye

1 There's something wrong with each of these sentences. What should you say to a visitor instead?

1. Sit down.
2. Did you have a good travel?
3. Would you like come to lunch with us?
4. Do you like a coffee?
5. 'This is Carl.' 'How are you?'
6. I look forward to see you again next month.

Listening

2 ▶9 Alessia, Karen and Peter work for RCS, an engineering company in Birmingham, UK. Carl Fischer, from Germany, is visiting the company. Listen to the three conversations and decide if these sentences are true (T) or false (F). Correct the false ones.

Conversation 1: Arriving
1. Alessia already knows Carl.
2. She offers Carl a drink.

Conversation 2: Meeting new people
3. Peter introduces Carl to the Chief Financial Officer.
4. Carl had a difficult trip.

Conversation 3: Time to go
5. Carl is going back to his hotel before he goes to the airport.
6. Peter and Carl will meet again in June.

3 ▶9 Listen again and tick (✔) the expressions you hear in the Key language section on page 13.

Pronunciation The schwa sound /ə/

1 ▶10 In fast spoken English, the words *to*, *a* and *was* are often pronounced /tə/, /ə/ and /wəz/. Listen to these exchanges and circle the words which have the schwa sound /ə/. There are seven.

1. **A:** Pleased to meet you!
   B: Pleased to meet you too!
2. **A:** Would you like a coffee or tea?
   B: A coffee, please!
3. **A:** Did you have a good trip?
   B: Not really. What about you?
4. **A:** How was your flight?
   B: Not too bad, thanks.
5. **A:** It was nice meeting you!
   B: Thanks, you too!

2 ▶10 Listen again and practise with a partner.

Get ready

4 What do you say? Practise responding to the following.

1. How do you do?
2. Nice to meet you.
3. Would you like tea or coffee?
4. This is Mr Lau, our Chief Financial Officer.
5. Did you have a good trip?
6. Have you had lunch?
7. Is your hotel OK?
8. It was nice meeting you.

Socialising 1   05

Key language for welcoming visitors

Greeting
A: Nice/Pleased to meet you.
B: You too.

Accompanying the visitor
Just follow me, please.
This is the meeting room.
Please have a seat.
Would you like a coffee or tea?

Introducing the visitor to others
Alessia: Carl, this is Peter. He's the engineer on this project.
Peter: Pleased to meet you, Carl. This is Karen. She's in charge of the finances.
Carl: How do you do?
Karen: How do you do?

Small talk
Did you have a good trip?
How was your flight?
Is your hotel OK?
Is this your first visit to Birmingham/Madrid?

Saying goodbye
A: It's late. I really must go.
B: Well, it was very nice meeting you.
A: Thanks, you too. I look forward to seeing you again in July, at the conference.
B: Yes, have a good trip. Bye!

TASK

5 **a** Work with a partner. You're expecting a visitor from another country.
   Student A: You're the host.
   Student B: You're the guest.
   First decide which town or city you're in, who the guest is, and why they've come.

   b Read the prompts below and take a minute to think about what you can say.

   c Act out the dialogue. When you've finished, swap roles.

Host	Guest
In the hotel	
It's 8.30 a.m. You're meeting your guest at their hotel. They arrive. Greet them.	Respond to your host's greeting.
Ask if they have had breakfast.	Answer. Ask if it's far to the office.
Answer. Suggest you take a taxi.	Agree.
In the taxi	
Ask your guest if they have ever been to your town/city before.	Answer. Make a comment about the place.
Agree/Disagree. Make a comment about the traffic/pollution in the town/city.	Compare the situation with your home town/city.
At the office	
Invite your guest to sit down and offer them a drink.	Answer. Ask where the toilets are.
Give directions.	Say thank you.
Introduce a colleague.	Greet the colleague.
After the meeting	
Invite your guest to stay for lunch.	Thank your host, but say it's late. Explain that you have to go.
Say goodbye.	Say goodbye.

06 Soft skills

Talk about your skills and abilities

Give advice

1. Businesspeople often need both 'hard skills' and 'soft skills' (sometimes called 'people skills'). Which type of skills does each definition describe?
   1. technical abilities, based on facts and knowledge
   2. personal qualities, such as being able to communicate well

2. Which of these are 'soft skills' and which are 'hard skills'?
   1. Giving presentations
   2. Knowing how to operate a computer program
   3. Working in a team
   4. Knowing how to drive
   5. Being flexible
   6. Understanding a balance sheet

3. Are soft skills important in your job? Why? / Why not?

Pronunciation Consonants: /z/, /s/, /ð/, /θ/

1. ▶11 Some English consonant sounds can be difficult to pronounce. Listen and repeat these words.

/z/	/s/	/ð/	/θ/
easy	sorry	they	think

2. ▶12 Decide which column of the table above these words should go in. Listen and check, then listen again and repeat.

   some   then   progressing   thing   say   other   soft   thin   sale
   organised   their   speak   languages   please   face
   with   presentation

3. Make some simple sentences with the words from Pronunciation Exercise 2 and practise saying them.

Key language for talking about skills

Abilities

I'm (quite/very) good at { us**ing** software. / help**ing** colleagues.

I can …
I'm able to …
I find it easy/difficult to …

Qualities for soft skills

to be { organised / confident / flexible

to be able to { work under pressure / take criticism / show initiative / have a positive attitude

Get ready

4. Look at the phrases for *Abilities* in the Key language section. Work with a partner. Talk about your abilities related to these topics.
   - managing your time
   - playing football
   - working in a team
   - making presentations
   - speaking foreign languages
   - singing

5 Complete these sentences with words or phrases for *Qualities for soft skills* in the Key language section.
1 There's never enough time in this job. I can't work under so much _____ .
2 He always gets angry if you suggest how he could work better. He can't _____ .
3 She always thinks she can do any job. She has a very _____ .
4 I find it difficult to manage my time. I'm not very _____ .
5 He always waits for somebody to tell him what to do. He doesn't show much _____ .
6 Change isn't a problem for her. She's quite _____ .

TASK

6 Do this questionnaire with a partner and find out about your soft skills.

Questionnaire

Make a note of your score for each question (①, ② or ③) and add up your score out of 60 at the end!

1 Are you good at explaining to other people how things work?
Yes ③   Usually yes ②   No ①

2 Do you think that other people (like bosses, colleagues, etc.) are stopping your career from progressing?
Yes ①   No ③

3 Is it OK to be rude to someone if they are not able to do their job well?
Yes ①   Usually ②   No ③

4 Can you always contribute during a discussion?
Yes ③   Usually ②   No ①

5 If you are organised and show initiative at work, you can be promoted.
True ③   Usually ②   False ①

6 Are you confident when you talk to people in authority?
Yes ③   Usually ②   No ①

7 Are you a good teamworker?
Yes ③   Usually ②   No ①

8 Do you ever volunteer for difficult jobs?
Yes ③   Sometimes ②   No ①

9 Are you happy to learn something new?
Yes ③   Usually ②   No ①

10 Do you say sorry when you've done something wrong?
Yes ③   Usually ②   No ①

11 Do you ask questions, even if others may think they're stupid?
Yes ③   Usually ②   No ①

12 Are you able to manage your time well?
Yes ③   Usually ②   No ①

13 Do you feel nervous if you enter a room full of people?
Yes ①   Sometimes ②   No ③

14 Do you try to keep good relations with your supervisors and boss?
Yes ③   Usually ②   No ①

15 Are you successful in what you plan to do (e.g. get a job, do training)?
Yes ③   Usually ②   No ①

16 Do you try to plan everything in advance?
Yes ③   Usually ②   No ①

17 Is it OK to do things that your boss might not agree with?
Any time ①   Sometimes ③   Never ②

18 Do you have a positive attitude at work, even when you're under pressure?
Yes ③   Usually ②   No ①

19 Do you talk to your colleagues and supervisors about your projects and successes?
Yes ③   Usually ②   No ①

20 Can you take criticism?
Yes ③   Usually ②   No ①

Score _____ /60 – For an analysis of your questionnaire score, look on page 84.

7 Do you think these kinds of test are useful? Why? / Why not?

Alternative task for pre-work students online

07 Presentations 1

Structure your presentation

1. Think of a good or a bad presentation you've seen. What was it about? Why was it a success or a failure?

2. Kato Lowit is the founder of a hi-tech engineering company. Today, he's making a presentation to some potential investors. Complete the gaps in his introduction with phrases from the Key language section.

> Good afternoon. I'm Kato Lowit and I'm the CEO of G-Frontier, a company which explores and develops the possibilities of that amazing material – graphene. My ¹_____ is to show you our latest and most exciting product and to invite you to invest $450,000 to help in its development. I know that some of you are not engineers, so if I get too technical, please ²_____.
> Now, ³_____ my presentation into three parts. First of all, I'll explain what the product is exactly; then ⁴_____ at its clear commercial potential; and finally, I'd like to tell you why this investment is so important to us and how you will be able to profit from it. ⁵_____ by looking at the material itself. What is graphene?

3. ▶13 Listen and check your answers.

Key language for starting presentations

Introducing yourself
Good morning, my name's Lorenzo Rossi and I'm manager of …

Presenting the subject
My aim today is to …
I'd like to talk to you today about …
I'm going to describe/present/explain the new …

Timing
This should take about 20 minutes.

Questions
If you have any questions, please feel free to interrupt.
Could you keep any questions to the end, please?

Describing the presentation structure
I've divided my presentation into three parts.
First / First of all, I'll show you …
Then / After that / Secondly, we'll look at …
Finally, we'll consider …

Start
Let's begin/start by looking at …

Presentations 1 07

Pronunciation Contracted forms

Contracted forms are often used in natural spoken English.

1 Complete the sentences below with these contracted forms.

I'd   let's   'll   've   I'm   don't   won't   you're

1 You _____ be able to access the program without a valid password.
2 After that, _____ like to talk about our sales figures.
3 _____ worry, you can ask questions at the end.
4 Before going on to my next point, _____ consider the figures.
5 If _____ happy with that, we can move on.
6 As you can see, I _____ highlighted three main points.
7 Finally, we _____ look at the results and come to our conclusions.
8 I work in sales and _____ in charge of marketing too.

2 ▶14 Listen and check. Then listen again and repeat.

Get ready

4 Work with a partner. Take it in turns to practise starting a short presentation of the company information in your file. Use the Key language.

Student A: Look at the information below.
Student B: Look at the information on page 85.

Student A
You don't need to give any of the detailed company information yet, you'll use that in Unit 8. For now, just:

- introduce yourself
- present the subject
- refer to timing and questions
- describe the presentation structure
- give the opening lines of your presentation.

Red Bull

Background
- An energy drink made by Austrian company Red Bull GmbH
- Company founded in 1984 by Austrian Dietrich Mateschitz and Thai Chaleo Yoovidhya
- In the early 1980s in Bangkok, Mateschitz discovered a cheap drink in a brown bottle called Krating Daeng (Thai for 'Red Bull'). It's now the most popular energy drink in the world.

Company statistics
- Number of employees: 11,886
- Countries available: 171
- First foreign market: Singapore (1989)

Sales
- Number of cans: 6.3 billion (4% increase on 2016)
- €6.28 billion turnover

Figures are for 2017

Reasons for success
- Innovative marketing campaigns aimed at young urban professionals
- Huge investment in sport sponsorship, e.g. Formula 1 team Red Bull Racing, Moto GP, New York Red Bulls football team, ice-hockey teams, rally teams
- Multimedia promotion through TV and new media

TASK

5 Give the first part of a presentation about an aspect of your work or about your company. Explain the structure of your presentation and how you would like to deal with questions.

Alternative task for pre-work students online

08 Presentations 2

Move forward and end a presentation

1 Read this advice about giving presentations and decide how useful you think it is.

	Good advice	It depends	Bad advice
1 Make sure there is a clear structure to your presentation and that the audience understands it before you begin.			
2 Slow down! Nervous presenters often speak too quickly.			
3 If you're nervous, focus on one person at the back of the room and speak to them.			
4 Ask the audience to keep their questions till the end.			
5 Keep moving around.			
6 Always try to tell a joke.			
7 Don't practise your presentation before you give it. It won't seem natural.			

2 Compare your answers in pairs.

Listening

3 ▶15 You're going to hear some more of Kato Lowit's presentation (see Unit 7). Listen and decide if these sentences are true (T) or false (F). Correct the false ones.

1 The product is a filter which produces salt water from drinking water.
2 The filter is made of graphene.
3 The product makes drinking water faster and more cheaply than its competitors.
4 Kato wants money to invest in a new factory.
5 Investors can be sure they will make a profit.

4 ▶15 Listen again and tick (✔) the expressions you hear from the Key language section on page 19.

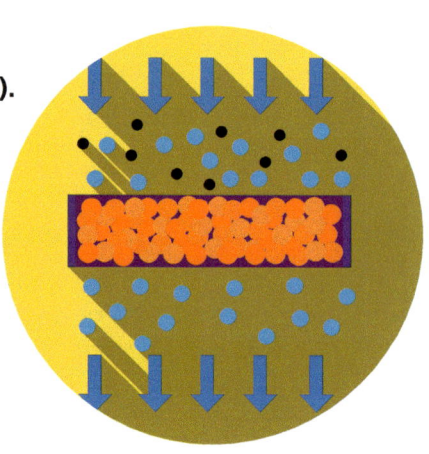

Presentations 2 — 08

Key language for taking forward and ending presentations

Moving on
Let's move/go on to …
Now we come to …

Giving consequences
so / as a result / because of this

Giving reasons
This is because …
The reason for this is …

Comparing and contrasting
however
in comparison with / compared to
on the one hand … on the other hand …

Focusing
Let's look at this in more detail.
What does that mean for us?

Summarising
To sum up, …
To summarise the main points, …

Ending
Finally, …
That brings me to the end of the presentation.
Thank you for your attention.
Any questions?

Pronunciation Linking /r/

The /r/ sound is often pronounced when it comes before a word that begins with a vowel sound.

1 ▶16 **Listen and repeat.**

We're‿offering a new product.
What does that mean for‿us?

2 **Draw the links between the /r/ sounds and the following vowels.**

1 They're out.
2 Your investment is important.
3 Their office is in Singapore.
4 You're older than me.
5 Where are they?
6 There isn't much time.

3 ▶17 **Listen and check. Practise saying the sentences.**

Get ready

5 Look back at the presentation information on Red Bull and Instagram again (pages 17 and 85). This time, use the Key language from Unit 7 and this unit to practise making short but complete presentations.

TASK

6 Give the full presentation of the one you began in Unit 7, Exercise 5. Remember to give your presentation a clear structure and use visual aids where possible.

Follow-up

7 Give each other feedback on your presentations. What was good about them? What could be improved?

09 Managing my time

1 **Read this text and discuss the questions below.**

> **Time and the Pareto Principle**
>
> In 1906, the economist Vilfredo Pareto noticed that 20% of the population in Italy owned 80% of the land. He also found that 20% of the pea plants in his garden produced 80% of the peas. Since then, people have seen similar patterns in other activities, including business. For example, do most of your sales come from a few of your products? Do you spend most time on things that make you the least money?

Talk about time management

1 Do you agree with this principle?
2 How do you organise your time at work?
3 How long is your 'to do' list for this week?

Listening

2 ▶18 **One way to understand how we spend our time is to create a chart showing our daily activities. Listen to Sachitar Kumar, the product manager for a cosmetics company, talking about her day. What are the two mistakes in her chart?**

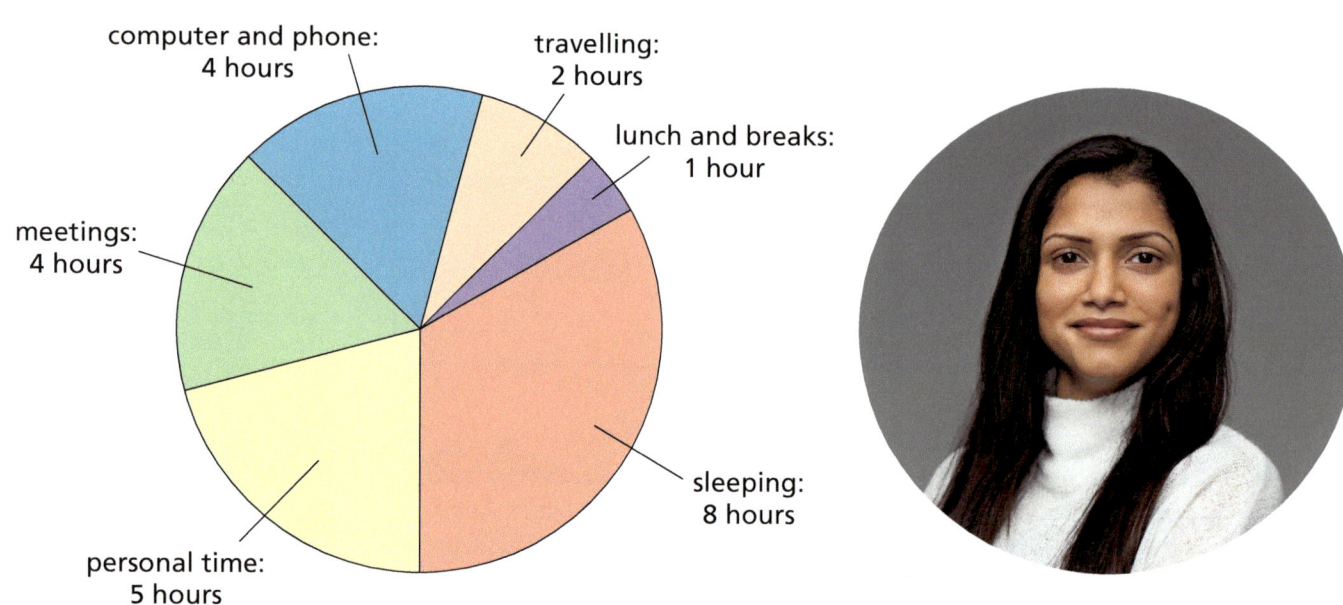

- computer and phone: 4 hours
- travelling: 2 hours
- lunch and breaks: 1 hour
- sleeping: 8 hours
- personal time: 5 hours
- meetings: 4 hours

3 **Work with a partner. How could Sachitar improve her time management?**

Example: I think she could/should …

Key language for talking about time	
to be late/early (for)	**Expressions with *time***
to delay	to spend time doing
to prioritise things to do	to take time to do
to meet a deadline	to waste time on something/someone
to finish by a date	a waste of time
to postpone an appointment	to save time
	most of the time
	to be on time

Managing my time 09

Get ready

4 **Complete these sentences using the correct form of words and phrases from the Key language section.**

1 We should finish the job _____ 18th January.
2 Yesterday, I _____ two hours writing the report.
3 I missed the train, so I was _____ for the meeting.
4 We've _____ too much time on that customer. He's not going to buy.
5 We can _____ time by taking the early flight.
6 It was a difficult project. It _____ six months to finish it.
7 They _____ the delivery by two weeks.
8 We need to _____ an August deadline.

Pronunciation Long and short vowels: /e/ and /eɪ/; /ɪ/ and /iː/

It's easy to confuse long and short vowel sounds.

1 ▶19 **These words have similar sounds. Circle the first word you hear in each pair. Then listen and repeat.**

1	date debt	5	bin been
2	get gate	6	waste west
3	will we'll	7	sleep slept
4	its eats	8	this these

2 **Now put the words into their groups and practise saying them.**

/e/ as in *spend*	/eɪ/ as in *late*	/ɪ/ as in *list*	/iː/ as in *be*

TASK

5 Use this circle to draw a pie chart like the one in Exercise 2 for your average working day and explain it to your partner.

6 Could you organise your time better? How?

Follow-up

7 **Work with a partner. Discuss these questions.**

1 Are you often late?
2 In your business, is it better to work quickly or carefully?
3 Do you take work home with you? Would you prefer to work from home? Why? / Why not?
4 Do you sometimes finish a job at the last minute, or ask to move a deadline?
5 How do you prioritise your 'to do' list?

Alternative task for pre-work students online

10 My procedures

Describe procedures at work

1 Greta Paget and Anna Braun started the international recruitment company Search Exec in 2015. These sentences describe how they began their business. Put them into the correct order.

   a   After finding an office, they bought furniture and equipment.
   b   Finally, they were able to do business.
   c   First of all, they prepared a business plan.
   d   Next, they rented an office where they could work.
   e   Then they borrowed some money from the bank to cover their start-up expenses.

2 What do you think the next steps were for Greta and Anna?

Listening

3 ▶20 Search Exec finds staff for its clients, who are usually Human Resources departments. Listen to Greta talking about their interview procedure. How many interviews are there in the procedure?

4 ▶20 Listen again and decide if these sentences are true (T) or false (F). Correct the false ones.
   1   The first interview is face to face or on the phone.
   2   During the first interview, they usually ask candidates about their last salary.
   3   In the second interview, candidates often meet the head of department.
   4   In the third interview, candidates meet people from Human Resources and Marketing.
   5   After attending the third interview, successful candidates will receive a written job offer.

5 ▶20 Listen again. Find and change the word/phrase that is different in each of these sentences.
   1   Our interview procedure depends on the position we're interviewing for, but there are generally four main steps.
   2   During this first interview, we usually ask the candidate in-depth questions about their work experience.
   3   The department head will tell the candidate about the responsibilities of the job and try to discover if they have the necessary skills to deal with these responsibilities.
   4   After that, they'll hear more about the pay.
   5   And finally, after waiting for four days, the successful candidate will receive written confirmation from the department head and a job offer.

My procedures 10

Key language for sequencing

first / first of all
then
after (waiting a few days)
before (offering the job)
next
so now
finally

Pronunciation Using pauses

1 ▶21 **Listen to these sentences. Where does the speaker pause to make the message clear?**

1 First of all, we arrange a face-to-face interview.
2 So we use either the phone or Skype.
3 Then if we call the candidate for a second interview, they're doing well.
4 After that, they'll hear more about the salary.
5 And finally, the successful candidate will receive a job offer.

2 ▶21 **Listen again and repeat with the pauses.**

Get ready

6 Look at these pieces of advice for a candidate before a job interview. Use the Key language to put them in a logical order.

Find out exactly where you have to go.
Make sure you aren't late.
Answer the questions clearly and honestly.
Find out as much as you can about the company offering the job.
Practise the interview with a friend.
Dress for the interview as you would for the job.
Prepare questions to ask during the interview.

TASK

7 Make notes on the stages of one or more procedures in your work, e.g. quality control, processing customers' orders, workplace safety, software installation, etc. Then describe the procedure(s) to a partner.

Example: First of all, we …

8 Discuss these questions with your partner.

1 Why are these procedures necessary?
2 Do things sometimes go wrong with them?
3 Do you think they could be improved? How?

Alternative task for pre-work students online

11 Stress

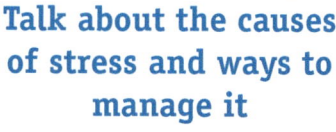

Talk about the causes of stress and ways to manage it

1 Describe what's happening in the pictures. When and why is the man under stress?

2 Do you think work is now more or less stressful than in the past?

Listening

3 You're going to hear a counsellor talking about stress. Before you listen, work with a partner. Which of these areas of our lives make us most stressed? Try to agree on the top three stress factors.

> children   health   holidays   meetings   money   parents   relationships
> time   travelling   work

4 ▶22 Now listen to the counsellor. Which three areas does she say make us most stressed? Are they the same as yours?

5 ▶22 Listen again and complete the gaps in this extract from the interview.

Interviewer: So what can happen ¹_____ of this stress?

Counsellor: The consequences can be serious. For one thing, you can develop health problems ²_____ people should really think more about it. [...] It's a question of managing your life better. For example, if you feel ³_____ because of work targets or deadlines, you ⁴_____ look at your schedule and ⁵_____ the most important things.

Stress 11

Key language for talking about stress

Stress
to be stressed   to be under pressure
to get stressed   to have a stressful job/time

Causes
He was stressed { because of / as a result of / due to } tight deadlines.

Consequences
He was stressed. { So / Consequently } he needed a holiday.

Solutions
You need to { look at your work–life balance. / talk to your doctor/bank/partner. / ask for help from colleagues. / organise your week's work. }

Pronunciation Silent letters

In English, not every letter is always pronounced. Sometimes there are silent letters:

knife /naɪf/ = silent *k*

half /hɑːf/ = silent *l*

▶ 23 **Listen to these words. Repeat them and circle the silent letters.**

talk   psychologist   straight   would   resign   listen   Wednesday
doubt   mortgage

Get ready

6 Make sentences from the table.

I feel much better	as a result of problems with her colleagues,	so she's decided to resign.
She woke up late	because of	Consequently, I often have headaches.
He's stressed	because she went to bed late,	pressure he's under at work.
She feels under pressure	as a result of the	my new schedule.
I get stressed	due to my work deadlines.	so she was late for work again.

TASK

7 Think about areas of your life that cause you stress (e.g. work, money, relationships). Place them on the 'stressometer' scale below.

Example: I get pretty stressed at work, so I'd put that at 80%.

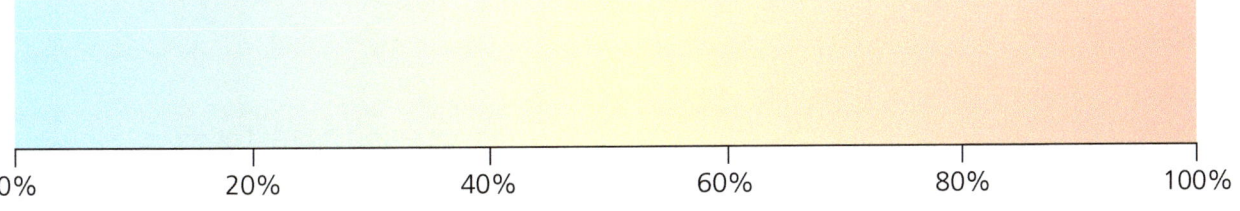

0%   20%   40%   60%   80%   100%

8 Tell your partner what you're stressed about; your partner can suggest action to take, and why.

12 Socialising 2

1 **Discuss these questions with a partner.**
   1 What was the last restaurant you went to?
   2 What food did you have there? Was it good?

Ask about and order food

Make conversation

The Rose Restaurant

Starters
Watermelon, prawn and avocado salad
Smoked salmon with onion and cucumber
Asparagus and leek soup

Main course
Roast beef with mushrooms and mashed potatoes
Grilled chicken with tomato and aubergine
Fried sea bass with spinach and almonds

Vegetarian
Baked red pepper with egg, olives and cabbage
Mixed leaf salad with mint, carrots, peas, garlic and a choice of dressings
Rice and mixed vegetables

Side dishes
Chips
Potatoes (mashed or boiled)
Rice (fried or steamed)

Dessert
Homemade cakes and ice creams
Fresh fruit salad: grapes, grapefruit, banana, kiwi, pear, raspberries, walnuts

Drinks
A selection of red, white and rosé wines
Still and sparkling water

Listening

2 ▶24 **Listen to a conversation between a waiter and two customers at The Rose Restaurant. Which of these orders is correct?**

   a **Man**: Asparagus and leek soup, grilled chicken with tomato and aubergine (with chips)
      Woman: Asparagus and leek soup, fried sea bass with spinach and almonds
      Drinks: 1 litre water (still)

   b **Man**: Asparagus and leek soup, grilled chicken with tomato and aubergine (with chips)
      Woman: Asparagus and leek soup, baked red pepper with egg, olives and cabbage (with rice)
      Drinks: 1 litre water (sparkling)

   c **Man**: Asparagus and leek soup, grilled chicken with tomato and aubergine (with chips)
      Woman: Asparagus and leek soup, fried sea bass with spinach and almonds
      Drinks: 1 litre water (sparkling)

3 ▶24 **Listen again and tick (✔) the phrases from the Key language section on page 27 that you hear.**

Get ready

4 **Match each cooking style (1–5) with its description (a–e).**

   1 baked   a cooked slowly in an oven, usually bread or cakes
   2 roasted   b cooked in water at 100°C
   3 fried   c cooked at a high temperature in an oven
   4 boiled   d cooked in hot oil
   5 grilled   e cooked over or under a great heat

Socialising 2 — 12

5 Match these foods (1–12) with items from The Rose Restaurant menu.

6 Work with a partner. Practise ordering dishes from the menu. If you don't know what something is, ask your partner. Use the Key language.

Key language for a restaurant

Arriving
We have a reservation.
A table for four, please.

Discussing dishes
What is (sea bass)?
(Sea bass) is a kind of (fish).
It's spicy/sweet/salty/hot.
It's cooked in …
Does it come with …?

Ordering
What would you like?
What do you recommend?
I'd like the …
I'll have the …
Could I have …?
I'll have the same.
Me too.
Would you like …?

Finishing the meal
That's enough for me, thanks.
That was delicious / very nice.
Could we have the bill, please?
Can I pay by credit card?

Pronunciation Diphthongs /eɪ/, /aɪ/, /əʊ/, /aʊ/, /ɪə/

1 Put these words in the correct column of the table below according to the sound of their diphthongs.

baked beer buy cake change fried grape grow hear I'll know main near now
our rice right same show shower smoked sound straight waiter wine

/eɪ/ as in *day*	/aɪ/ as in *fine*	/əʊ/ as in *no*	/aʊ/ as in *out*	/ɪə/ as in *here*

2 ▶25 Listen and check, then practise saying the words.

TASK

7 Work in groups of three. Two of you have just arrived at The Rose Restaurant. Talk about the food on the menu, then choose and order your meal. At the end, pay and leave. Take turns to be the waiter/waitress.

8 What are you going to talk about during your meal? Make your own conversation or choose from the 'Conversation menu'.

What do you think of …?
Do you like …?
Have you ever been to …?
Have you heard about …?
Have you seen …?

Conversation menu
- the restaurant
- business
- holidays
- fashion
- sport
- books
- food
- events in the news
- family
- another person
- films
- music

13 Problem-solving

Use the language of problem-solving

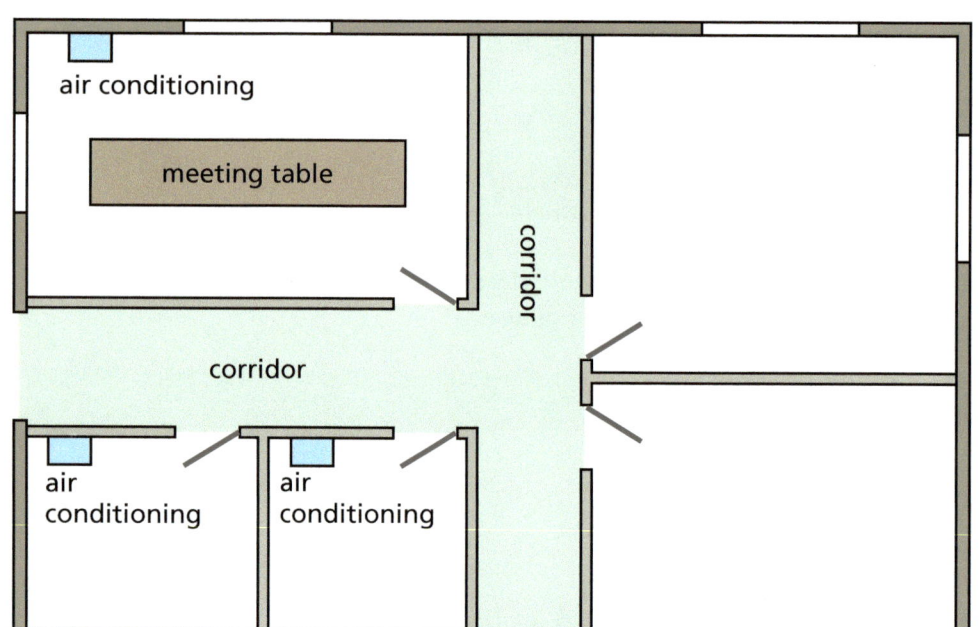

1. Your company has just moved to new premises. You're the office manager, responsible for placing the six staff below in the five offices in the plan above. Read what the staff have said and discuss with a partner where you're going to put them.

> I'd like my own quiet office in a corner of the building if possible.

Kushal, Senior Manager

> I really need an office with air conditioning.

Julia, Senior Manager

> I don't mind really, but please … I don't want to share an office with Dolores. She's always on the phone and she's so loud!

Pavel, Junior Manager

> I don't mind sharing an office, but not with Valentino, please. A room with two windows would be nice.

Dolores, Assistant

> I'd like a room with a big table, for me and Dolores.

Valentino, Junior Manager

> I need a large, bright, comfortable room with a meeting table.

Su, Department Director

2. Compare your solution with another two colleagues. Decide which solution is the best.

Listening

3. ▶26 A family retail business has a problem. You're going to hear part of a meeting between members of the family and their accountant, Margaret. Read these two summaries, then listen and decide which one best describes the situation.

   a As the costs of creating and running a website are high, their father doesn't want one for the family business. One of the sons thinks their father should retire now, but the others don't agree. The accountant thinks they should show their father some good websites and explain how to use them. The others all agree.

   b Their father doesn't want the business to go online because he thinks it will cost too much. One member of the family suggests asking him to retire, as he's 63 years old. The others don't agree. The accountant suggests showing him proof that creating a company website can improve sales.

28

Problem-solving 13

Get ready

4 Join the sentences in the two columns below using different phrases for *Giving reasons and results* from the Key language section.

Examples: Their father didn't want to set up a website **because of** the cost.
As the cost was high, their father didn't want to set up a website.

Problems
There are delivery delays to customers.
Our computer system is very slow.
I was late for the meeting.
I haven't had a salary increase for three years.
We're spending too much on supplies from the USA.
People often don't follow projects through from beginning to end.

Reasons
It's ten years old.
There is a very high staff turnover.
Business hasn't been good.
The high price of the dollar.
We often don't have the goods in stock.
I missed the train.

Key language for solving problems

Giving reasons and results
We didn't buy it **because** the quality was poor.
We didn't buy it **because of** the poor quality.
The reason why we didn't buy it was the poor quality.
As the quality was poor, we didn't buy it.

Offering solutions
Why don't you …?
You should …
You could …
What about (–ing)?
I suggest (–ing)

5 Suggest solutions to the problems in Exercise 4 using phrases for *Offering solutions* from the Key language section.

Pronunciation Sentence stress

1 Underline the important words to stress in these sentences.
Their father didn't want to set up a website because of the cost.
As the cost was high, their father didn't want to set up a website.

2 ▶27 Listen and check.

3 ▶28 Listen to and repeat these sentences.
As we **often** don't have the **goods** in **stock**, there are **delivery delays** to **customers**.
Our **computer system** is very **slow** because it's **ten years old**.
I **missed** the **train**, so I was **late** for the **meeting**.
We're **spending** too **much** because of the **high price** of the **dollar**.

TASK

6 List some problems you have at work.

7 The family in Exercise 3 used these steps to arrive at a solution.
1 Identify the problem.
2 Identify the causes.
3 Brainstorm solutions.
4 Choose the best solution.

Work with a partner to solve your problems from Exercise 6 using the same steps.

Alternative task for pre-work students online

14 Travel

1 **Discuss these questions with a partner.**
- How did you get here today? How long did it take you?
- How do you usually travel?
- Do you prefer to travel by car, train, bus, plane or ship? Why?
- Have you visited another country? Why did you go there? How did you get there? How long did it take to get there?
- Which country would you most like to visit? Why?

Use the language of travel

Ask for information

Key language for travel

Asking for information
Do you know what time the next train to (Moscow) is?
Can you tell me what time (flight LA562) arrives?
Could you tell me why there's a delay?

Talking about journey times
How long does it take to get to (Berlin) by (train)?
It takes about (two hours).
How long does it take you to get to work?
It takes me about (20 minutes).

Travel verbs

to get { a train/plane
to (*a place*)
on/off a train/plane/bus
into/out of a car/taxi }

to go by train/plane/car
to arrive in (a city/country)
to arrive at (the airport/station/hotel)
to change trains
to book a ticket

to buy a { single/return ticket (BrE)
one-way/round-trip ticket (AmE) }

Get ready

2 **Indirect questions are more polite. Look at the questions for *Asking for information* in the Key language section. Use the phrases in column A to change the direct questions in column B into indirect questions.**

A	B
Do you know …? Can you tell me …? Could you tell me …?	1 When does the train leave? 2 Where is the station? 3 Which train do I have to get? 4 What time is it? 5 How does this ticket machine work? 6 Which terminal does the flight leave from?

Pronunciation *have*

1 ▶29 **Listen. Notice the different pronunciation of *have* in these two sentences.**
　1 Do I **have** to change trains? /hæf/
　2 How much luggage do you **have**? /hæv/

2 ▶30 **Listen and repeat the six sentences that you hear.**

Travel 14

3 Use the *Travel verbs* from the Key language section to say what's happening in these pictures.

TASK

4 ▶31 You're going from your hotel in London to Victoria Station and then to Gatwick Airport to catch flight LA562 to Los Angeles. Work with a partner. Decide what you would say in each situation, then compare your responses with the recording.

1 You want to fly to Los Angeles from London. You call the airline for information: *Hello. I'd like …*

2 You want to know the arrival time of your flight: *Could you tell me what time …?*

3 Ask the hotel receptionist how you can get to Gatwick: *Can you …?*

4 You don't know which terminal at Gatwick your flight leaves from. You call the airport.

5 Now you're in the Underground station, but you're lost! Ask somebody which train you have to take to get to Victoria Station.

6 You're talking to the same person. Ask if you have to change trains.

7 You get to Victoria Station. In the information office, you ask for the time of the next train to Gatwick.

8 You also want to know how long the journey to Gatwick is.

9 In the ticket office, you want to know the price of a single ticket to Gatwick.

10 You're at Gatwick Airport. At the check-in desk, the clerk asks you how much luggage you have.

11 The clerk asks if you would prefer an aisle seat or a window seat.

12 Your boarding card says departure is from Gate 32, but you can't find it. Ask somebody.

5 Work with a partner. Go through situations 1–12 in Exercise 4, taking it in turns to respond and get to your destination.

15 My career

Talk about your education and career

1 Use the phrases below (a–e) to say how much you agree with each of these sentences (1–5).
1. You can't expect to get a job for life these days.
2. It's more important to make a lot of money than to enjoy your job.
3. It's better to be self-employed than to work for somebody else.
4. These days, your online connections are more important than your CV.
5. In my country, it's not what you know, it's who you know.

a I totally agree. (100%)
b I agree on the whole. (75%)
c I'm not sure. / It depends. (50%)
d I disagree on the whole. (25%)
e I totally disagree. (0%)

Key language for talking about education and career

I was born in (*place*) in (*year*).
I live in …
I went to school in …
My secondary/high school was …
I went to college/university in (*place*) from (*year*) to (*year*).
I've got a degree/diploma in (*subject*) from (*institution*).
I worked for (*company/organisation*) from (*year*) to (*year*).
I left my last job because …
Now I work for (*company/organisation*) as (*job title*).
I've been in this job since (*date*) / for (*period*).
Now I'm looking for a job as …
In the future, I'm going to … / I'd like to … / I hope to … because …

Pronunciation The schwa sound /ə/

1 ▶32 Listen to the words *to*, *a*, *from* and *for* in these sentences. How are they pronounced?

Where did you go **to** school?
I've got **a** degree in Modern Languages **from** Bologna University.
I worked **for a** company in Milan **for** two years.

In fluent spoken English, the words *to*, *a*, *from* and *for* are often pronounced /tə/, /ə/, /frəm/, /fə/.

2 Highlight the schwa sounds in these sentences.
1. I'm going to look for a new job.
2. She comes from Berlin.
3. I went to school in France.
4. Are you going to stay in this job for long?

3 ▶33 Listen to and practise saying the sentences.

My career 15

Get ready

2 **Match the questions about education and career (1–10) with the answers (a–j).**

1 Where and when were you born?
2 Where do you live?
3 Where did you go to school?
4 Did you go to university?
5 What qualifications do you have?
6 What work experience do you have?
7 Why did you leave that job?
8 Did you find another job?
9 Are you going to stay in this job for long?
10 How long have you been in this job?

a I left because I wanted to find a position with more responsibility. There weren't any possibilities of promotion in that company.
b I like the work, but I'm going to look for a position as Logistics Manager next year.
c After university, I started work in a logistics company as an assistant to the European Manager. Then I left that job …
d I went to Hawksmoor School in Watford.
e I've got a Bachelor's degree in Modern Languages.
f I was born in Elstree, UK, on 4th April, 1995.
g Yes, I went to university in Bologna.
h Yes, I now work as Logistics Co-ordinator for ITC Trading in Milan.
i I live in Milan.
j For two years.

3 🔊 34 **Now listen to someone taking part in a survey in the street and check your answers.**

TASK

4 **Work with a partner.**

Student A: Use the questions in Exercise 2 to interview Student B. Help them with Key language when necessary.
Student B: Close your book and answer Student A's questions.

When you've finished, change roles and do the interview again.

Alternative task for pre-work students online

16 My company

Talk about the history and activities of a company

- Allianz
- BP
- Gazprom
- eBay
- IKEA
- Samsung
- Unilever
- Toyota

1 What do you know about the companies listed above?
- Where are their head offices?
- What do they do?
- Do you know anything about their history or the people behind them?

Listening

2 ▶35 You're going to hear descriptions of four of the companies in Exercise 1. Which companies are described?

3 ▶35 Listen again and identify the company described in each of these sentences.
1. You can insure your car with them.
2. It started in America.
3. There are more than 400,000 employees worldwide.
4. It has its group headquarters in Liechtenstein.
5. It builds houses as well as ships.

Key language for presenting your company

My company produces/manufactures …
The services the business provides are …
The company started in (year).
It was founded in (year).
It started as a …
It's based in …
The headquarters are in …
It has (three) sites/offices/factories/plants.
It has operations in …
There are (350) employees.
The company employs (350) people.

At the moment, the company is { doing well. / doing quite well. / not doing so well. }

34

Pronunciation Past simple verb endings

1 ▶36 Regular past simple verb endings can be pronounced in three ways. Listen to the three verbs in the table and repeat.

/ɪd/	/d/	/t/
started	lived	developed

2 ▶37 Listen to these words and put them in the correct column of the table above.

based   diversified   employed   expanded   fired   founded   hired
manufactured   produced   wanted   worked

3 ▶37 Listen again and repeat.

Get ready

4 Reorder the words to make questions.
1 produce? | does | What | company | the
2 the | services | company | provide? | What | does
3 it | based? | Where | is
4 company | many | got? | How | sites | has | the
5 it | begin? | When | did
6 started | Who | it?
7 it | start? | How | did
8 develop? | it | How | did
9 many | there? | How | employees | are
10 moment? | performing | is | it | at | How | the

5 Work with a partner. Ask each other the questions in Exercise 4 to get information about two of these companies: eBay, Allianz, Samsung or IKEA. You can use audio script 35 on page 92 to help find the answers.

TASK

6 Use the questions in Exercise 4 to ask each other about your own companies or organisations. Use the Key language to help you.

Follow-up

7 Discuss these questions with a partner. Give reasons for your answers.
1 Would you prefer to work for a large multinational or a small local company?
2 Do you think some large multinational companies have too much power?
3 Is there a particular company you would like to work for?
4 Would you like to work in a family business?
5 If your company operated internationally and asked you to move abroad, would you go?

Alternative task for pre-work students online

17 Our products and services

1 Which brand / company name of these products and services do you use most often?

> toothpaste   mobile network operator   hairdresser   airline
> supermarket   computer

Describe your products and services

2 Why do you choose these?

Listening

3 You're going to hear some descriptions of products and services. Before you listen, look at the photos. Which products and services do you think they represent?

4 ▶38 Now listen and match the descriptions (1–4) with four of the products and services from Exercise 3 (a–f).

Key language for describing products and services

Describing products
They're made of steel.
It's for cleaning windows.
They come in (three) colours.
It's composed of (three) parts.
There are a range of sizes.
It's (one metre) long/wide/high.
The packaging is cardboard.
The retail price is ($5.99).

Describing qualities
The advantage of this is the speed of delivery.
It's cheap compared to other services.
This allows you to work faster.
This offers more benefits.

Our products and services 17

Get ready

5 You can use *for* + *–ing* to talk about the use or purpose of things. Ask and answer about the objects in these photos.

Example: **A**: What's this for?
B: It's for mixing food.

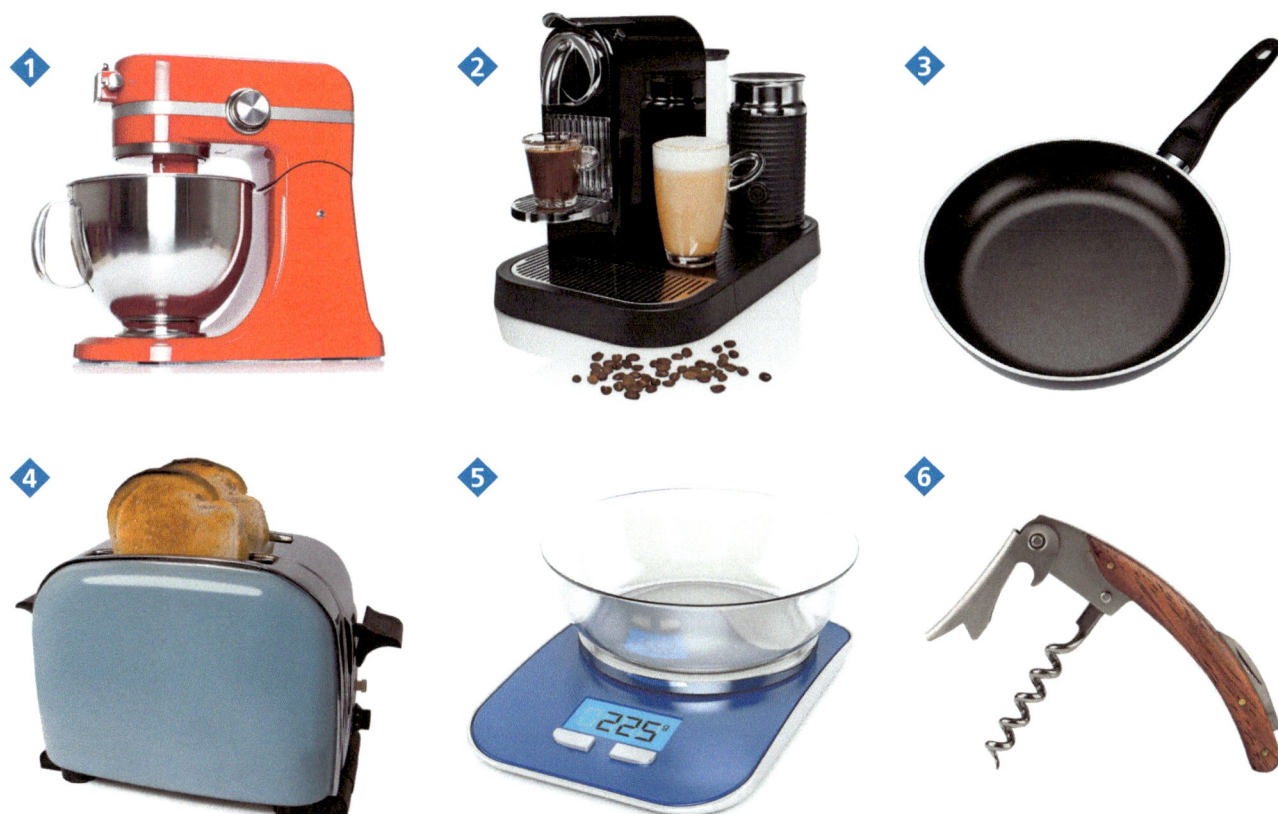

6 Work in a group. Take it in turns to think of a product or service. The others will ask you *Yes/No* questions to find out what it is.

Examples:
Is it a product or a service?
Can you buy it in a shop?
Is the price more than $50?
Is it made of plastic?
Have you ever bought one of these?
Do you use it for cooking?

TASK

7 Describe your company's products or services using these prompts.

Product	Service
what it's for	what it's for
appearance: size, weight, etc.	who it's for
packaging	customer benefits
price	development
range	price
customer benefits	

Alternative task for pre-work students online

18 Our company structure

1 Read this text and discuss the questions below.

The Danish company Oticon is one of the world's most important manufacturers of hearing aids. In 1988, the company hired Lars Kolind as CEO. Soon after, he announced to the employees the beginning of a new style of management called 'the spaghetti organisation'. The changes he made included: no formal hierarchy, self-organised project teams responsible for projects from start to finish, no formal job titles and no employee to have their own desk or office.

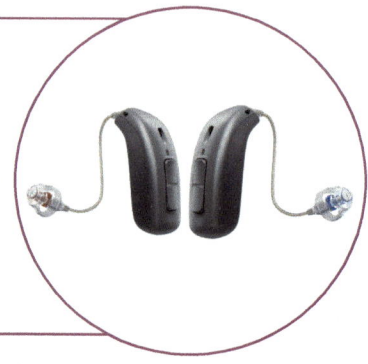

Describe your organisation

1 Why do you think Oticon's organisation is like spaghetti?
2 Would you like to work in an organisation like this? Why? / Why not?

Listening

2 ▶39 Moira Spencer works for Realgame, a company which produces video games. You're going to hear her talk about her company's organisation and her role in it. Listen and complete the gaps in the organogram below with the words from the box.

| Assistant   CEO   Chief of Finance   Operations   plc   Public Relations |

3 ▶39 Listen again and answer these questions.
1 Where is Realgame's parent company?
2 Does Realgame sell abroad?
3 What is the board of directors responsible for?
4 Who do the department directors report to?

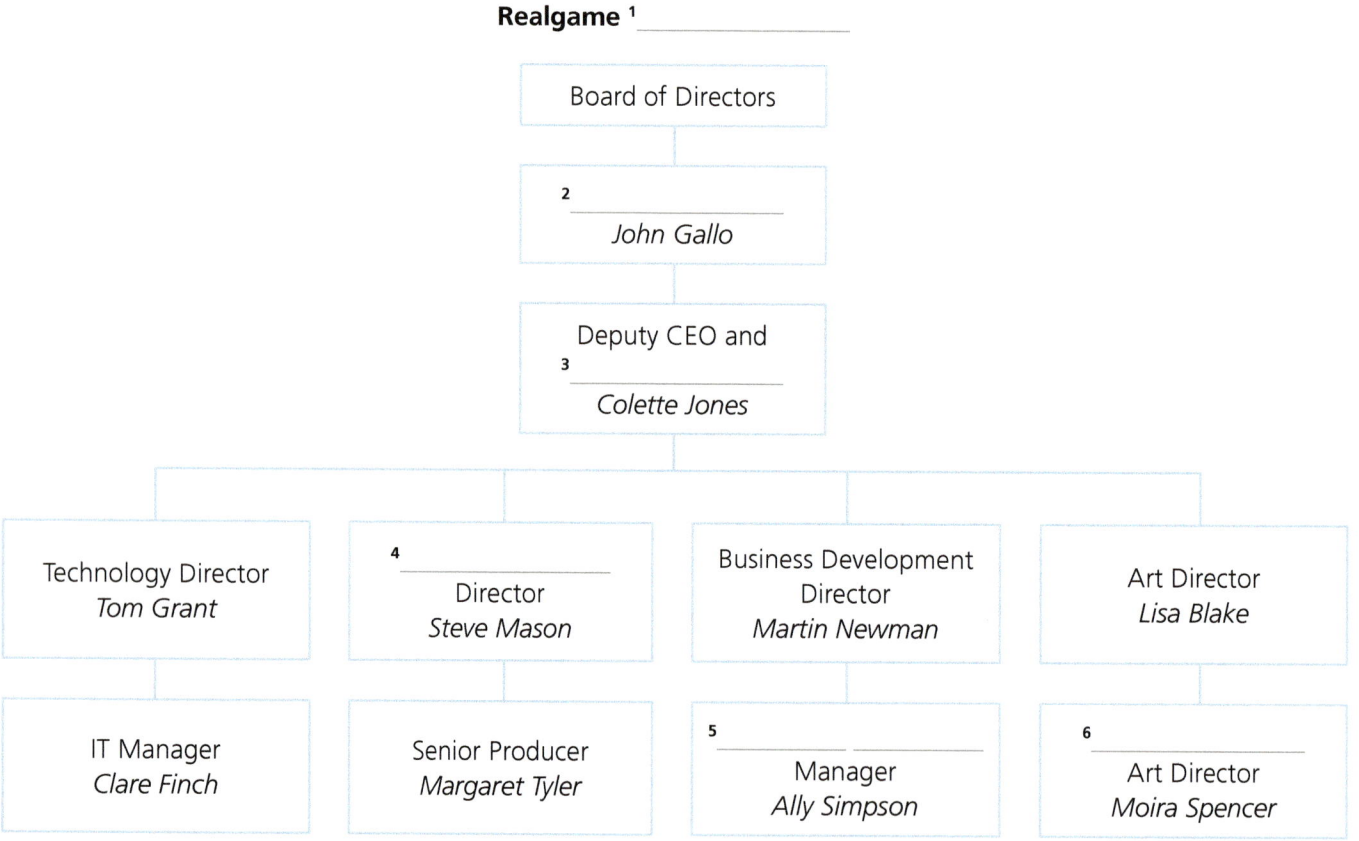

Our company structure 18

Pronunciation Word stress

▶40 **Look at these jobs. The stress patterns are marked above them: stressed syllables are marked O and unstressed syllables are marked o. Listen and repeat.**

o O o
1 a-ssist-ant

O o o
2 ma-na-ger

O o O o O o
3 chief fi-nan-cial o-ffi-cer

o O
4 ca-shier

O o O o o
5 soft-ware pro-gramm-er

O o O o o o O o
6 busi-ness de-vel-op-ment di-rec-tor

o O o o o
7 co-or-di-na-tor

O o o O o O o o
8 hu-man re-sour-ces ma-na-ger

Key language for describing your organisation

Ways to describe your organisation
The *parent company* is in …
There are (three) *subsidiary companies*.
The *head office* is (located) in …
The company is divided into (four) *business areas*.
I work in the (sales) *department*.
Tom Grant is *responsible for* …
Mr/Dr/Ms … *reports to* Mr/Dr/Ms …

People
Personnel, employees and *staff* are often used to mean the same thing, although *staff* usually support management, for example the *administrative staff*.

Top positions
- The company's shareholders elect the *Board of Directors*.
- A *Managing Director* in the UK normally has the title of *President* in the United States.
- A *Chairperson, Chairman* or *Chairwoman* is the head of a company, but is not always involved in its day-to-day management.
- The *Chief Executive Officer (CEO)* often describes the top position in large companies with several business units.

Get ready

4 Use the Key language to describe the organisation of Realgame. Look at audio script 39 on pages 92–93 for help if necessary.

TASK

5 **What kind of organisation do you work for? Draw your company or department's organogram.**

6 **Describe your organogram to your partner.**
   Example: At the top, there is …
   The organisation is divided into three …
   Mr … is responsible for …
   I report to …

Alternative task for pre-work students online

19 Connecting online

Make connections online

1 **Talk about your online communications with a partner.**
   1 Do you prefer communicating by telephone or over the internet?
   2 How many e-mail addresses do you have? (If you have more than one, explain why.)
   3 What social media do you use (e.g. Facebook, Twitter, Instagram)? Why?
   4 How important is an online presence (website, Twitter feed, social media, etc.) to your company?

Listening

2 **You're going to hear some e-mail and website addresses. Before you listen, match the symbols (1–9) with their names (a–i).**

   1 .   a dash/hyphen
   2 -   b backslash
   3 /   c dot
   4 \   d underscore
   5 #   e asterisk
   6 [ ]   f hash(tag)
   7 @   g forward slash
   8 *   h at
   9 _   i square brackets

3 ▶41 **Now listen and write down the seven different addresses and websites that you hear.**

Key language for presenting your company

Connecting

You can …
- contact me at samabell@filmore.com.
- get hold of me on Facebook or via e-mail.
- message us through Facebook.
- follow us on Twitter.
- call me on Skype at …

Our website is / Our web address is …
It's all lower case / upper case.
That's all one word.
There's a problem: our website/e-mail/server is down.

Checking

Can you spell that, please?
Could you repeat that?
Is that a dash or an underscore?
Can you read that back to me?
Can I just confirm that?

Connecting online 19

Pronunciation Saying the alphabet

We can group alphabet sounds like this:

/eɪ/ as in *way*	/iː/ as in *we*	/e/ as in *bell*	/aɪ/ as in *my*	/əʊ/ as in *home*	/uː/ as in *shoe*	/ɑː/ as in *far*
a, _____	b, _____	f, _____	_____	_____	_____	_____

1 ▶42 Work with a partner and complete the table above with the other letters of the alphabet. Then listen, check and repeat the groups.

2 Which are the vowel sounds? Practise saying these.

Get ready

4 Write these things down, then practise saying them with a partner.
- an e-mail address
- a website address
- a Twitter account
- a Facebook or Instagram account

TASK

5 Work with a partner. Take turns making phone calls and leave two of these messages (1–4). Use the memos below to note the two messages you hear. Don't forget to use the Key language to check that you've written the addresses correctly.

1 Ask a supplier to send e-mail confirmation of a meeting next Thursday.
2 Suggest a customer follows your company on Twitter to get details of a new promotion with price discounts.
3 Tell a colleague to message you on Facebook or Instagram with details of a conference you will both attend next month.
4 Tell a client about your new website. They can see new products, order online, track their orders and ask questions in real time with live chat.

MESSAGE

From: _____
Date/time: _____
_____
_____
_____
_____

MESSAGE

From: _____
Date/time: _____
_____
_____
_____
_____

20 Meetings 1

Give opinions, agree and disagree in meetings

Let's go round the table for your views on this, then I'll tell you what I've already decided to do.

1 Do you agree or disagree with these statements? Why?
1. The meetings I attend usually achieve their objectives.
2. They take too much time.
3. They always follow a correct procedure.

Listening

2 You're going to hear some extracts from a company meeting which has these three points on the agenda. Before you listen, decide which should be dealt with first. Order them according to their priority (1–3).

  a The policy of your company has been to develop teamwork. Bonuses are paid to teams for their performance. However, some employees are complaining that they do most of the work in the team, while some others do very little, but they all get the same bonus.

  b There is going to be an international trade fair in Hawaii in November which concerns your business. Representatives from Production, Finance, Sales and Marketing, R&D and Human Resources have all said they want to go. There are only three places available. Who should go?

  c In the last year, one of your biggest customers has become a very slow payer. Your terms of payment are 90 days, but they hardly ever pay within 120 days. This is beginning to cause serious cashflow problems.

3 ▶43 Now listen to the extracts. Is the order of points the same as yours?

4 ▶43 Listen again and complete the gaps in these extracts with expressions from the Key language section on page 43.

Chairperson:	They're beginning to cause us problems, because they're so slow to pay. ¹_____ . Tom?
Tom:	We have to be very careful with them. We can't just call and tell them to pay now, they're too important to us. Unfortunately, ²_____ wait.
Chairperson:	… while others who don't get the bonus too. ³_____
Su:	Yes, we should look at each person's work. ⁴_____ have a system of individual bonuses, so you receive a bonus for the work you do?
Hans:	No, ⁵_____ . The idea is to encourage teamwork …
Tom:	Well, one of the people who's preparing our stand there should go, I think.
Su:	⁶_____ , but really, as James said, we have to look at our aims. I mean, we want to sell, don't we?

42

Key language for opinions

Asking for opinions
Let's go round the table for views on this.
What do you think, Tom?
Do you agree, Hans?
Any ideas?

Giving opinions and suggestions
In my opinion, …
I think we should …
Why don't we …?

Agreeing and disagreeing
Agree
Yes, I totally agree.
I think Tom's right.
Yes, good idea!

Agree in part
I agree on the whole, but …
I see what you mean, but …
That's true, but …
Mm. Maybe.

Disagree
No, I don't agree because …
(I'm afraid) I can't agree with that.
I disagree completely.

Pronunciation Identifying and using affirmatives and negatives

1. ▶44 **Listen to five sentences and circle the verbs you hear.**
   1. could / couldn't
   2. weren't / were
   3. can't / can
   4. shouldn't / should
   5. are / aren't

2. ▶44 **Listen again and repeat the sentences.**

3. **Write some sentences with the words from Pronunciation Exercise 1 and dictate them to your partner.**

Get ready

5. **Work in small groups. You're going to have a meeting to discuss the agenda in Exercise 2. Study the Key language. Decide who's going to be the chairperson and begin your meeting.**

TASK

6. **Plan an agenda of issues to discuss concerning your own workplace(s) and hold a meeting to exchange opinions.**

Alternative task for pre-work students online

21 Figures

Work with numbers

1 How do you say the following?
1. the date you were born
2. the date today
3. the number of days in a year
4. the price of a one-bedroom flat in your area
5. the population of your town
6. the population of your country
7. your phone number
8. the percentage of men in your workplace

Key language for numbers

100	a hundred
1,000	a thousand
1,000,000	a million
1,000,000,000	a billion
286	two hundred and eighty-six
0.64	zero/oh point six four
0889 723 (tel.)	oh/zero, double eight, nine, seven, two, three
26%	twenty-six per cent
1st March	the first of March
23rd April	the twenty-third of April
2019 (year)	twenty nineteen / two thousand and nineteen

+ plus   – minus   × multiplied by   ÷ divided by   = equals

¼ a quarter   ⅓ a third   ½ a half   ¾ three quarters   ¹⁄₁₀ a tenth

Differences between British and American English

	AmE	BrE
0	zero	zero/oh
467	four hundred sixty-seven	four hundred and sixty-seven
11.6.21	November sixth, 2021	the eleventh of June, 2021
2006	two thousand six	two thousand and six

Get ready

2 ▶45 **Say these numbers aloud. Then listen and check.**

a	0.25	e	1,840	i	12,201,382
b	100	f	23,687	j	8,000,000,000
c	130	g	489,592		
d	401	h	4,427,309		

3 ▶46 **Say these figures aloud. Then listen and check.**

a	€68.39	f	49%	k	⅓
b	$298.38	g	100%	l	½
c	£5,493.93	h	Tel.: 01273 566934	m	¾
d	03/06/2015 (BrE)	i	66 kph	n	¹⁄₁₀
e	03-06-2015 (AmE)	j	¼		

Figures 21

Pronunciation Word stress in numbers

1 ▶47 Listen and repeat the pairs of numbers. Is the stress on the first or second syllable in each one?

A	B
sixteen	sixty
thirteen	thirty
fourteen	forty
fifteen	fifty
seventeen	seventy
eighteen	eighty
nineteen	ninety

2 Work with a partner. Say one of the words from Pronunciation Exercise 1. Your partner must say if it's from column A or column B.

Listening

4 ▶48 Listen and correct the figures where necessary.

1 ¥386
2 4,860
3 ↗136,500
4 $25 ↗ $30
5 ↘14%
6 269 ÷ 2 = 133.5
7 ⅓
8

TASK

5 Work with a partner. Compare all the numbers on your invoices, without looking at each other's documents, and find six differences between them.

Student A: Look at the invoice below.
Student B: Look at the invoice on page 85.

6 There's a mistake in the calculation of one of the invoices. What is it?

JK Hardware   23 Blackstone Road   Blackstone   East Sussex BT6 8KD   Tel. 01273 55982

Carlton Plc
48 Thames Street
London W1D 1LA

Invoice no. 634

Account no.	Invoice date:
BRN887	22/10/19

Product code	Description	Quantity	Unit price	Total
PD15486	F23 tablet computer	45	£387.42	£17,433.90
KJ15	X90 back-up drive	37	£59.90	£2,216.30
Subtotal				£19,650.20
Less 10% discount				£1,965.02
Total due				**£17,685.18**

22 Trends

Describe change in figures

1 Look at this graph. Which line do you think is the correct one? Why?

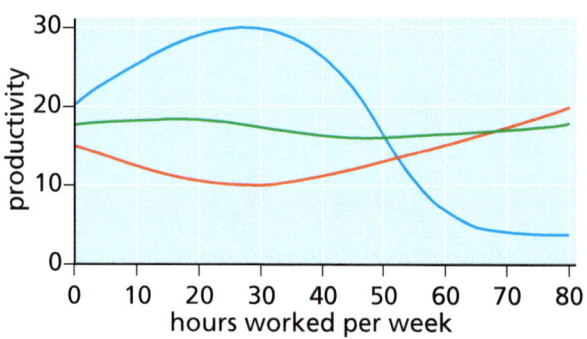

Listening

2 ▶49 Listen to a sales executive presenting the results of motorbike sales over the last six months. Complete the bar graph.

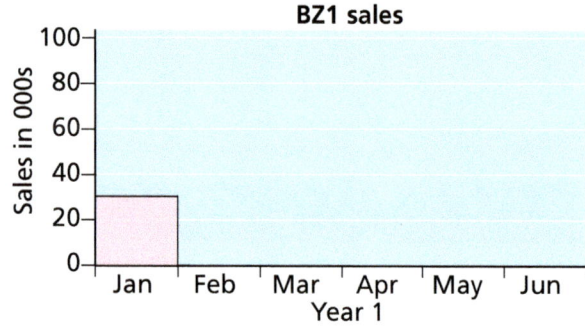

Key language for describing trends

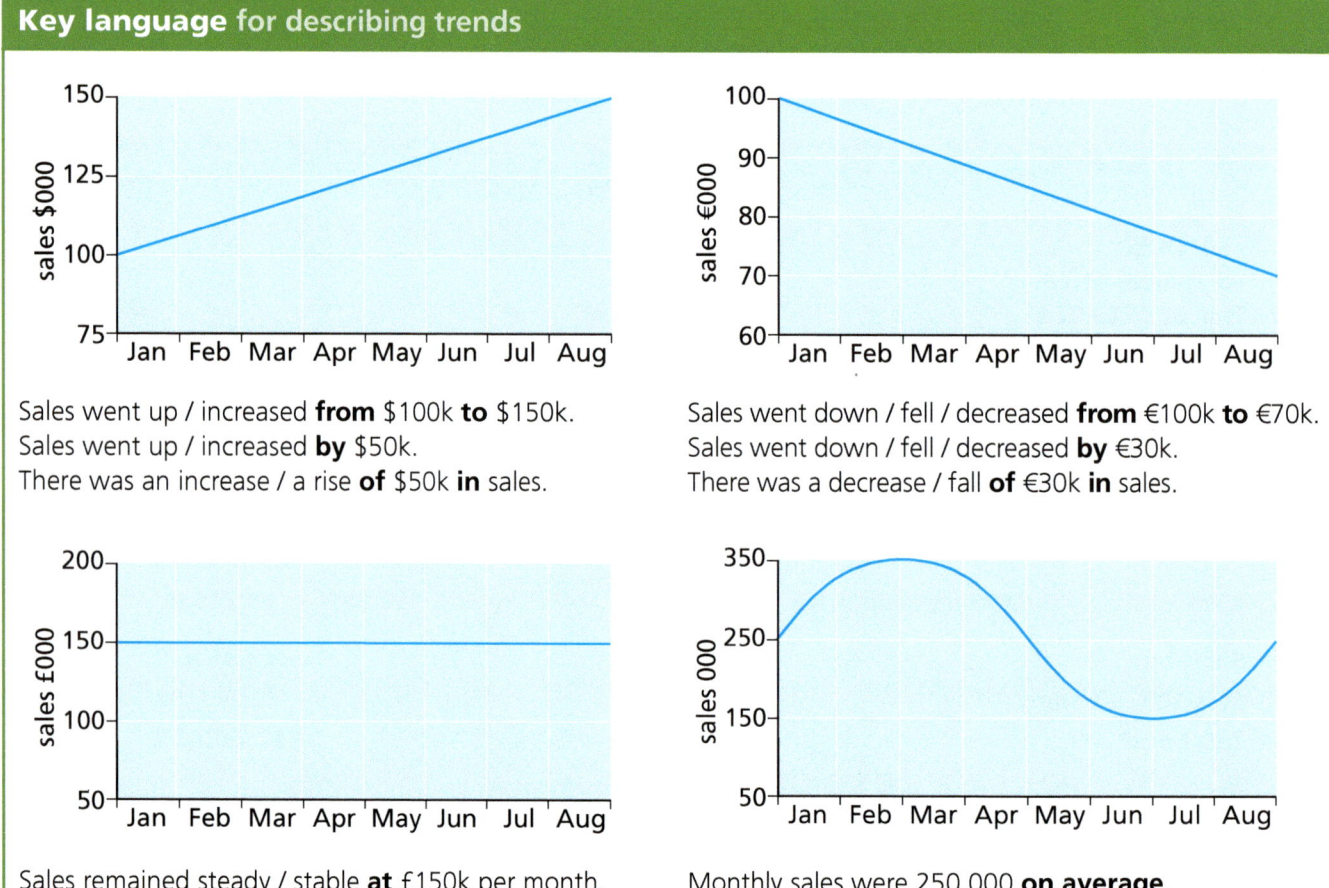

Sales went up / increased **from** $100k **to** $150k.
Sales went up / increased **by** $50k.
There was an increase / a rise **of** $50k **in** sales.

Sales went down / fell / decreased **from** €100k **to** €70k.
Sales went down / fell / decreased **by** €30k.
There was a decrease / fall **of** €30k **in** sales.

Sales remained steady / stable **at** £150k per month.

Monthly sales were 250,000 **on average**.

Trends 22

Pronunciation Linking words

1 ▶50 **Listen and notice how some words are linked to others. This happens when one word ends with a consonant sound and the next begins with a vowel sound.**

Sales went‿up by 10%.
Production went down‿on‿average.
There was‿a fall‿in the figures.
Sales‿increased‿in January.
Percentages remained stable‿at 6%.

2 ▶50 **Listen again and repeat.**

Get ready

3 Put these verbs and verb phrases of movement in the correct column of the table below.

| dropped   fell   has fallen   has risen   increased   remained stable   rose   stayed constant   went down   went up |

↘	→	↗

4 **Work with a partner.**
   Student A: Use the Key language to describe the movements on this graph to Student B. It shows historical changes in the price of gold in the UK.
   Student B: Listen to Student A and complete the graph on page 86.

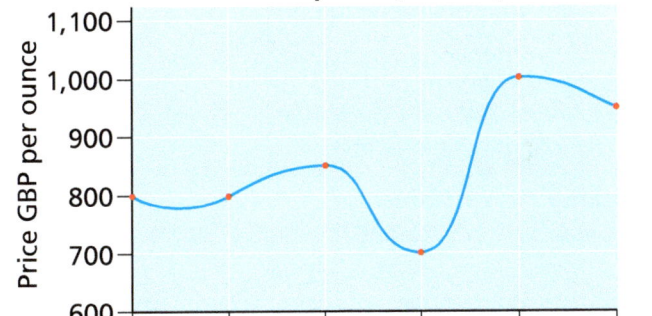

5 **Work with the same partner.**
   Student A: Listen to Student B and complete this graph.
   Student B: Turn to page 86.

TASK

6 **Prepare to describe trends from your work in recent years, such as production, sales, prices, profits, etc.**

Alternative task for pre-work students online

47

23 Socialising 3

Entertaining at home

1 Which of these statements do you think are true?
1. German businesspeople like to separate their home life from their work.
2. Chinese businesspeople believe socialising with foreign visitors outside work helps to build trust.
3. Guests should leave their shoes by the door in Asian countries and in Scandinavia.
4. In Russia, it's polite to accept all the food and drink your host offers you.

Key language for entertaining at home

Arriving
Hello! Come in. Lovely/Nice to see you again.
Let me take your coat.
Shall I leave my shoes here?
I've brought you this little present.
That's very kind of you.

First things
Come through to the living room.
Make yourself at home / comfortable.

Offering/responding
Can I get you something to drink? / Would you like a …?
Yes, could I have … , please?
How do you like your tea/coffee?
One sugar, please – no milk.

Making conversation
Did you have any trouble finding the way here?
No, it was easy. I used the sat-nav.

Preparing to leave
Could you tell me where the toilet/bathroom is, please?
Thank you very much for the tea/lunch, etc.
It's getting late. I really should go.
It was nice to see you.
You must come to my house the next time you're in …

Listening

2 You're going to hear a conversation between a host and her guest. Before you listen, look at the Key language and write H (host) or G (guest) after each phrase, according to who is talking.

3 ▶51 Now listen and check your answers.

Pronunciation Backchaining and intonation

▶52 Listen and repeat the parts of these sentences you hear. Copy the intonation.
1. Nice to see you again.
2. That's very kind of you.
3. Make yourself at home.
4. How do you like your coffee?
5. Thank you very much for the tea.
6. It's getting late.

Socialising 3 | 23

Get ready

4 Read this conversation and think of what you can say in each gap. Then practise it with a partner.

Host: Hello! Come ¹_____ . Lovely to see ²_____ . Let me take ³_____ .
Guest: Shall I leave ⁴_____ ?
Host: Yes, please do.
Guest: I've brought ⁵_____ .
Host: Oh, that's very ⁶_____ . Come ⁷_____ the living room. Make yourself ⁸_____ .
Guest: Thank you.
Host: Can I get ⁹_____ ? Some tea, ¹⁰_____ ?
Guest: Yes, please. I ¹¹_____ tea.
Host: Sure, how ¹²_____ it?
Guest: ¹³_____ .
Host: Did have any trouble ¹⁴_____ here?
Guest: No, it was ¹⁵_____ . I used the sat-nav … Could you tell me where ¹⁶_____ ?
Host: Yes, sure, it's ¹⁷_____ .

Guest: It's ¹⁸_____ late. I really ¹⁹_____ .

5 Write three questions or comments to make further conversation with a guest or host.

Examples: Have you always lived in Tokyo/Jakarta/Bombay/São Paulo, etc.?
What a beautiful room/picture/dress!
How long have you lived in this flat/house?
Do you like this area?

TASK

6 Work with a partner. Practise this situation.
Student A: You're the guest visiting Student B's home.
Student B: You're the host.

Follow-up

7 Discuss these questions.
1 Do people usually invite business guests home in your country?
2 Do you invite clients to your home? Why? / Why not?
3 How do you prefer to entertain business guests? Why?
  - inviting them to your home
  - inviting them to lunch at a restaurant
  - inviting them to dinner at a restaurant
  - taking them for a cup of coffee
  - inviting them to a club or other event (e.g. a concert, the theatre)
  - taking them to the company restaurant for lunch

Alternative task for pre-work students online

24 The marketing mix

1 The 'marketing mix' helps us to understand key points when marketing a product. The diagram shows the 'four Ps' of the marketing mix.

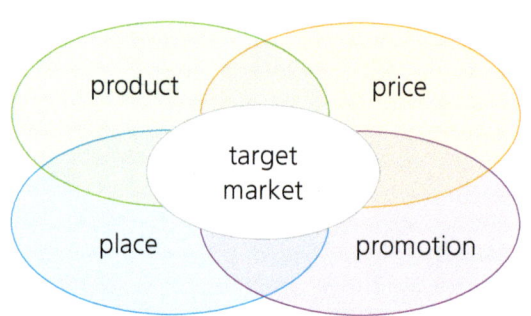

Talk about your company's marketing

In which of the four Ps are these speakers having problems?
1 'The customer will think that, because it's only $12, it must be low quality.'
2 'The cost of the free gift is much too high compared to the expected increase in sales.'
3 'Young people just don't go to the kind of store we're supplying.'
4 'It looks boring to me. The packaging doesn't catch the eye at all.'

2 Think of an example you know where a mistake was made with one of the four Ps. Tell your partner or teacher about it.

Listening

3 ▶53 Listen to marketing executive Mansour Mohamed talking about the fast-food chain McDonald's and the marketing mix. Which of the four Ps does he say is the most important for the company?

4 ▶53 Listen again and circle the correct parts of the sentences.
1 They want to know which items the customer wants to *see / eat* on the menu.
2 Some products might be popular *today / tomorrow*, but not *tomorrow / today*.
3 … they advertise *on / in* TV, online, in the cinema, using *in-store / on-store* promotions and loyalty schemes.
4 … when they decide *on / about* a price, they know it's important not to go too *low / high* …
5 … they reach around *42 / 52* million customers a day. Nearly *50% / 60%* of the US is less than *three / two* minutes away from their nearest McDonald's …

Key language for the marketing mix

Product
to meet/satisfy needs
a well-known brand
to brand a product
packaging
product lifecycle

Place
store (*AmE*), shop (*BrE*)
(car) dealer
trade customers
online sales
distribution channels (*the ways the product reaches the customer*)
retailer (*sells to the general public*)
wholesaler (*sells to other distributors or retailers*)

Price
value for money
price-sensitive
a discount
a competitive price
high/low price

Promotion
advertising online / in the press / on TV / on radio / on billboards
advertising campaign
direct marketing
special offers and free gifts
social media (*social networking sites and blogs*)
loyalty schemes

The marketing mix 24

Get ready

5 Match the sentence halves.

1 The product meets
2 Customers trust
3 The packaging
4 Tea goes through a long distribution
5 We advertise on
6 Buyers can purchase
7 Our clients are not very price-
8 Our prices are low
9 We sell retail to customers online

a and wholesale to supermarkets and other stores.
b channel from farmer to retailer.
c compared to the competition.
d customers' needs internationally.
e goods direct from our website.
f is bright and attractive.
g the web and in the press.
h sensitive, so we often raise our prices.
i well-known brands.

6 Work with a partner.

Student A: Think of a well-known brand or product in terms of the four Ps. Write a few notes about it.

Student B: Try to guess the name of the product or brand. Write a few questions to ask Student A.

Example: **A:** This is a very old brand. You can find it in most supermarkets.
B: Is it a kind of food?

Pronunciation Word stress in phrases

Many marketing terms are made up of two nouns or an adjective and a noun. We say the words in the phrases with an equal stress.

Read these sentences aloud, paying attention to the stress in the phrases in bold.

1 **Market research** helps us decide on the menu.
2 We can promote our products with **in-store promotions** and **loyalty schemes**.
3 McDonald's uses **competitive pricing** when deciding its policy.
4 Asda is always **price-sensitive** when it comes to its goods.
5 We have various **distribution channel**s all over the country.
6 We prefer to do **direct marketing** in the traditional way.
7 You can find **special offers** every weekday.
8 Coca-Cola is one of the world's **best-known brands**.
9 Its **advertising campaigns** have always been original.

TASK

7 Prepare to give a short talk on your organisation's marketing activities. Choose two or more of the four Ps in the table and use the questions as a guide. Make notes, then give your talk.

Product	Price
Describe the product.	Is the customer price-sensitive? Why?
What needs does it satisfy?	How do your prices compare to the competition's?
How and where do customers use it?	Do you offer discounts?
Place	**Promotion**
Where can customers find your product?	Where and how do you advertise?
If they buy from a store, what kind of store?	What other ways do you use to promote your product?
Can they buy direct from your website?	Do you use direct marketing?
What distribution channels are there?	

Alternative task for pre-work students online

25 Selling

Study the language of selling

Persuade people to buy

1. Research has shown that five of the words below are the most powerful in persuading people to buy. Which do you think they are?

   because   cheap   free   instant   new   quality   special   you

2. As a customer in a shop, do you like to have advice from sales assistants, or do you prefer to decide on your own? Why?

Listening

3. ▶54 Listen to part of a conversation between a sales rep and a customer and answer these questions.
   1. Which of the products below (a, b or c) does the customer order?
   2. How many does she order?

a headphones

b earbuds

c mobile phone cases

4. ▶54 Listen again and tick (✔) the words and phrases you hear for *Persuading* from the Key language section.

Key language for selling

Persuading
I'd like to offer you …
Let me tell you about …
If you … , I'll …
Have you thought about …?
Why don't you try it?
It might be a good idea to …
Would you give me two minutes to tell you about …?
Compared to others on the market, …
They're very popular.
The advantages of … are …

Responding
Sorry, I'm not interested.
I'll think about it.
Maybe. What's your best price?
OK, that's a deal. / That's agreed.

Sales vocabulary
price list
list price
an invoice / to invoice
to offer a discount
sales force/target/volume
salesperson / sales rep
to sell out
unit price
to close a deal
sales pitch / sales presentation
wholesale
range of goods

Pronunciation Sound vs spelling

1 Which of these pairs of words have the same pronunciation?

1 price	prize	6 by	buy
2 sell	sale	7 knows	nose
3 right	write	8 tell	tail
4 it	eat	9 whole	hole
5 weight	wait	10 work	walk

2 ▶55 Listen and check.

Get ready

5 Match these definitions (1–9) with phrases from the *Sales vocabulary* in the Key language section.

1 to suggest a reduction in price
2 the price on the list
3 the list of prices
4 to send someone a bill
5 to sign the sales contract
6 the price of each article
7 to sell all of your goods, including stock
8 a salesperson who represents the company
9 all the products available

6 Try to sell one of the products below (a–e) to a partner. Before you start, think of:

- how it can help your customer
- what's new about the product
- what advantages it has compared with the competition
- the price you can offer.

a a smartphone that produces 3D holographic images
b a high-speed document scanner
c super-efficient solar panels
d high-tech pro golf equipment
e a slimming programme

TASK

7 Work with a partner. Try to sell one of your company's products or services to your partner.

Follow-up

8 Discuss which of the sales channels in the diagram below you would use to sell these products and services.

car insurance   electronic goods   fresh fish   haircuts   soft drinks   tractors

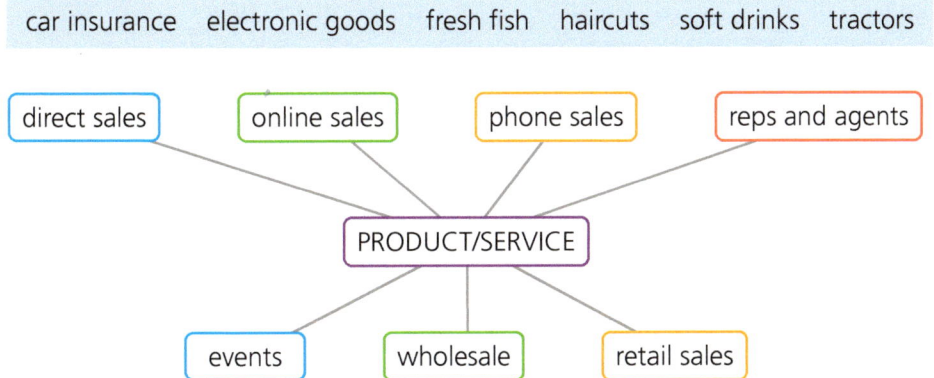

9 Which of the sales channels in Exercise 8 are used most in your business? Why?

Alternative task for pre-work students online

26 Know your customer

1 What do you know about these retailers? What are their customers like?
- Harrods • Primark • Hollister • Gucci

2 Which of these are most important to you when you buy clothes? Why?

comfort   label   look   price   quality

Describe typical customers

Create a customer profile

Listening

3 You're going to hear descriptions of three customers. Before you listen, look at these photos. Work with a partner to describe the customers using the Key language to help you.

a

b

c

d

4 ▶56 Now listen and match the three customers described with the photos in Exercise 3. There is one photo you won't need.

Key language for talking about your customers

What are your customers like?

Types
clients (usually for services)
customers (usually for goods)
corporate customers

Age
about 30 years old
from 20 to 40
teenaged/middle-aged/elderly

Gender
They're typically/mainly women.

Family status
married with children
single

Nationality and geographical area
They come from Asia / all over the world.
They're from villages/towns/cities.
They're urban/rural.

Jobs
They're professionals / skilled workers.
They have manual jobs.
They're retired.
They earn high salaries.

Income
low income
middle income
high income / big spender

Know your customer 26

Get ready

5 Match these questions (1–2) with the correct answer (a–b).
1 What do your customers like?   a They like quick delivery.
2 What are your customers like? b They're mainly middle-aged women.

6 Choose the best answer (a or b) for each question.
1 What's she like?
   a She likes fast cars.
   b She's about 30. She's very quiet, but clever.
2 What do they like?
   a They like high-quality products.
   b They're high-quality products.
3 What's the service like?
   a It's slow.
   b They like it.
4 What don't you like about the new car?
   a No, I don't like it.
   b The price.
5 What was the presentation like?
   a It was a bit boring.
   b It liked them.

Pronunciation Unstressed words

Many grammatical words aren't usually stressed. They're spoken faster, using the schwa and contractions.

▶57 **Listen to these sentences and practise saying them. Be careful of the pronunciation of the words in italics.**
1 *Can* you tell me about your customers?
2 *They're* mainly women *and* they work *at* home.
3 *They're from* cities.
4 Where *do* they live?
5 This group is aged *from* 20 *to* 40.
6 *Does* she work *for a* bank?

TASK

7 Create a customer profile for one of your products or services. Make notes using these topics, then give a short talk describing your customers.

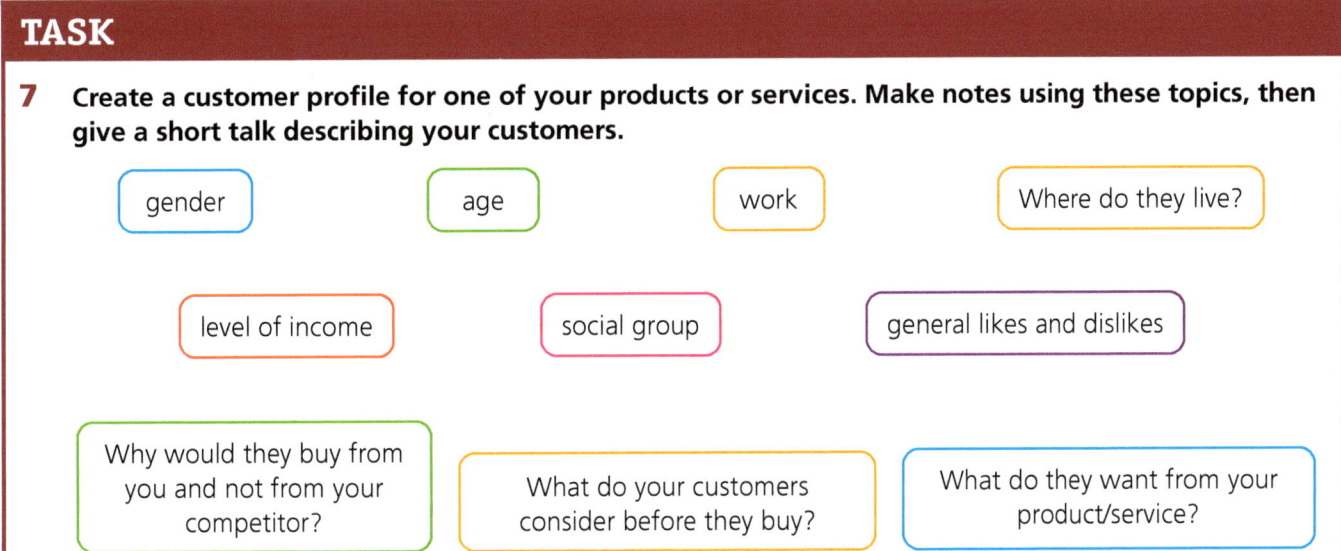

Alternative task for pre-work students online

55

27 Our business online

Talk about internet use

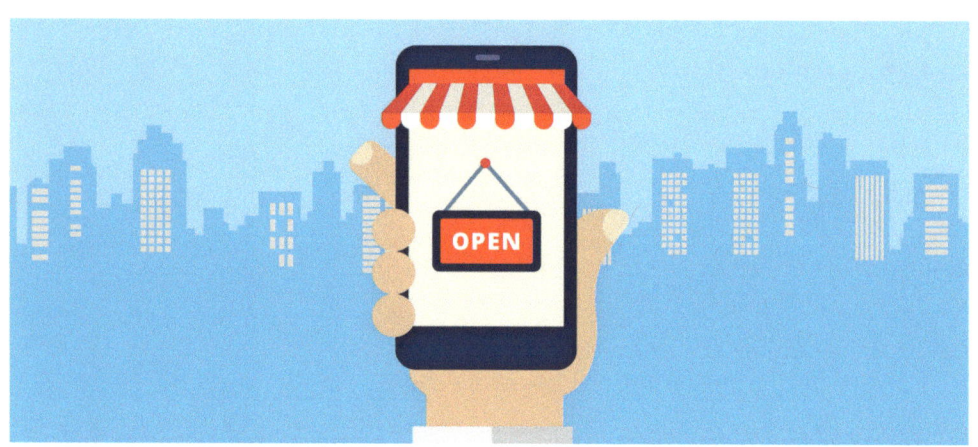

1 A recent survey measured the percentage of 16–75-year-old shoppers in the Netherlands who bought things online. Match the goods and services (1–7) with the percentages (a–g).

1 clothes and sports items
2 electronic equipment
3 financial products and services
4 groceries, cosmetics, cleaning products
5 software
6 travel tickets and holiday accommodation
7 tickets for events

a 6%
b 24%
c 49%
d 23%
e 45%
f 12%
g 58%

Source: CBS

2 What kind of products do you think don't sell well online? Why?

Key language for business online		
e-commerce	to download/upload a file	to design
B2B (business to business)	user-friendly	to set up
B2C (business to consumer)	to scroll down a page	to visit } a website
to go online	to click on a link	to log onto
homepage	to order over the net	to browse
web page	to access a database	
to search for information		

Get ready

3 Complete these sentences with expressions from the Key language section.
1 Customers can visit the company website and _____ product information.
2 Those with a password can _____ the site.
3 The site's very _____, and I think it's good advertising, too.
4 We've _____ our own website.
5 Customers _____ the net and we deliver to their workstations.
6 The sales team can _____ the database for customer information.

Listening

4 You're going to hear three people talking about how they use the internet in their work. Before you listen, look at the uses of the internet for business in the first column of the table on the next page. Which of these do you think are the most important?

56

Our business online 27

5 ▶58 Now listen and tick (✔) the uses they talk about.

	Anja Winter confectionery *Belgium*	**Gabriela Silva** management consultancy *Argentina*	**Joe Turati** pizza delivery *United States*
buying or selling	✔		
database			
public relations, providing information			
training staff			
marketing, finding new customers			
customer service			
doing research			
communicating with employees			
watching competitors			
advertising jobs			

6 ▶58 Listen again and decide if these sentences are true (T) or false (F). Correct the false ones.

1. Anja says that customers can follow the progress of their orders by logging on with a password.
2. Gabriela thinks the internet is more important than personal contact.
3. Gabriela often contacts her staff by Skype and e-mail.
4. Joe's customers are mostly businesspeople.

TASK

7 Make brief notes under these headings and discuss with a partner.

How I use the internet in business	How I use the internet in my free time

Follow-up

8 How do you think the use of the internet will change in the future?

Alternative task for pre-work students online

28 Meetings 2

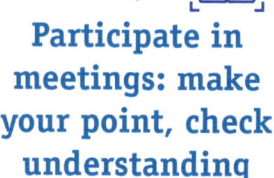

Participate in meetings: make your point, check understanding

1. The sentences below are from the minutes of a meeting. Complete them with the words and phrases in the box.

   | absent | adjourned | apologies | attended | bring forward |
   | held | point | postpone |

   1. The meeting was _____ on 15th April at Head Office.
   2. Mr Schmidt _____ the meeting by teleconference.
   3. Ms Megat was _____, but sent her _____.
   4. _____ five on the agenda was not discussed.
   5. The meeting _____ for lunch at 12.30.
   6. It was agreed to _____ discussion of new import duties to the next meeting on July 16th.
   7. It was decided to _____ the August meeting from the 21st to the 10th.

Listening

2. You're going to hear part of a meeting in which this issue is being discussed. Before you listen, decide what your opinion about it is.

   Some of your sales staff have been complaining about one of the sales representatives, Margot Lee, who regularly gives large gifts to important customers. Margot is your most successful sales executive.

3. ⏵59 Now listen and decide if these statements are true (T) or false (F). Correct the false ones.
   1. Margot has been the most successful sales executive for three years.
   2. There is a company rule which says that sales executives can't give presents with a value of more than $150.
   3. One speaker thinks that they should consider the profit that Margot makes for the company.
   4. At the end of the discussion, they decide to stop Margot giving expensive gifts to customers.

4. ⏵59 Listen again and tick (✔) the expressions you hear from the Key language section.

Key language for meetings

Asking for repetition and clarification
Sorry, could you repeat that last point again?
What do you mean by …?

Interrupting
Could I just say something here?
Sorry to interrupt, but …

Reacting to interruptions
If I could just finish …
As I was saying …

Delaying a decision
Well, that depends on …
Yes, that's a possibility. / Yes, maybe.
Let's wait until we have more information.

Returning to a point
Coming back to what I was saying, …
Going back to the point about …

Checking understanding
So what you're suggesting is …
So you're saying … Is that right?
Does that mean …?

Brainstorming opinions
We could …
How about …(–ing)?
What about …(–ing)?

Stating preferences
I'd prefer to have … than …
The main advantage of … is …

Meetings 2 **28**

Pronunciation Similar vowel sounds

1 ▶60 **Listen and notice the vowel sounds in these words.**
/æ/ ran   /ʌ/ run

2 ▶61 **Listen to and repeat these pairs of words.**
1 cat   cut
2 fan   fun
3 match   much
4 began   begun
5 drank   drunk

3 ▶62 **Listen and notice the vowel sounds in these words.**
/e/ end   /æ/ and

4 ▶63 **Listen to and repeat these pairs of words.**
1 men   man
2 head   had
3 said   sad
4 any   Annie
5 bed   bad

5 **Work with a partner.**
Student A: Say one of the words in the lists in Pronunciation Exercises 2 and 4.
Student B: Point to the word..

Get ready

5 **Complete these sentences using phrases from the Key language section.**
1 You want to finish what you were saying. *If I …*
2 You want to return to a point. *Going …*
3 Somebody else is speaking, but you want to say something. *Could I …*
4 You want to check that you've understood. *So what …*
5 You didn't understand what the last speaker said. *Sorry, …*
6 Say that you'd prefer to delay a decision until you have more information. *Let's …*

TASK

6 Your company has to cut its training budget for next year by 20%. Look at the table below showing the courses that were held last year, their share of the budget and their satisfaction rating. Think about the changes that you would make. Then meet as a group to decide on the budget for next year. Use the Key language from this unit and Unit 20.

	% of budget	Satisfaction rating last year
Computer software	20	★★★★
Sales techniques	5	★★★★★
Languages	10	★★★
Using the phone and e-mail	10	★★
Induction training of new recruits	5	★★★★
Health and safety	5	★★★★
Management training	20	★★★
Personal training: persuading and influencing people	10	★★
Improving quality	10	★★
Marketing	5	★★★★

7 Plan an agenda of issues to discuss concerning your own workplace and hold a meeting using the Key language from this unit and Unit 20.

Alternative task for pre-work students online

29 Production

Describe production processes

1 How many of the words in the Key language section on page 61 can you identify in the picture?

2 What's happening in the picture?

Listening

3 You're going to hear a description of the process for creating an object using a 3D printer. Before you listen, look at these pictures and decide what the correct order should be.

The printer is programmed for the materials to make the object.

The material is hardened by a laser.

A 3D image of the object is designed on a computer.

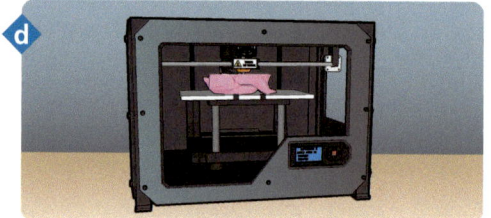

The object is created in layers.

The information is sent from the computer to the 3D printer.

4 ▶64 Now listen and check your answers.

Key language to describe production

The **workers** usually work in teams.
Raw materials are stored in the **warehouse**.
Products are put together on **assembly lines**.
A **conveyor belt** passes with **semi-finished products**.

Industrial robots are used in thousands of applications.
The **finished goods** are **packed** before delivery.
Goods on **pallets** are transported by **fork-lift trucks**.
The **machinery** is maintained by **mechanics**.

Pronunciation Word stress

⏵65 **Look at these word families. Listen and mark the stressed syllables in each word. Which word in each group is different? Practise saying the words.**

1 produce (v.)   product   producer   production   productive
2 compete   competition   competitor   competitive
3 advertise   advertising   advertisement

Get ready

5 Descriptions of production processes often involve passive verb forms.
   Active: *The computer **sends** the information.*
   Passive: *The information **is sent** by the computer.*
   How many passive sentences are there in the Key language section?

6 Change these sentences into the passive form.
   1 We send the goods by lorry.
   2 She sends the order by e-mail.
   3 They make the cars in Warsaw.
   4 We check the quality of the raw materials in the factory.
   5 They sell the fruit in supermarkets.
   6 They pack the goods in cardboard boxes.

7 Work with a partner. You're going to explain to each other how two products are made.
   Student A: Look at this page.
   Student B: Turn to page 86.

   Student A
   Describe how striped toothpaste is made.
   • two or three colours | make individually
   • two separate compartments at the top of the tube | fill with colours
   • rest of the tube | fill with white toothpaste
   • the white and colours | mix when the tube | squeeze

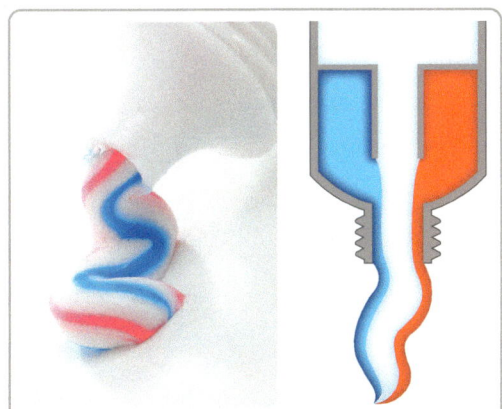

TASK

8 Make notes on production or service processes at your work. Then describe them to each other.
   First … then … after that … finally …

Alternative task for pre-work students online

30 Orders and delivery

Describe the steps from enquiry to delivery

1. You work for an international delivery company. What would you do in these situations?
   1. You want to ship 50,000 computer screens from Shanghai to Sydney.
   2. You need to send a mobile phone from Berlin to Tokyo.
   3. You have 12 tons of fresh cheese in a refrigerated lorry travelling from Italy to Sweden. The refrigerator has broken down in Munich. It's summer, and you think the cheese has three hours before it's spoilt.
   4. You have to transport a racehorse called Uncle Benny, worth €70m, from Hong Kong to Dublin. Uncle Benny doesn't like flying.

Listening

2. You're going to hear a description of the sale and delivery of some printers. Before you listen, look at the boxes and circle which you think is the correct choice in each step (1–8).

1	2	3	4	5	6	7	8
enquiry	quote €180	check stock	14 days	dispatch	invoice	lorry	customer
warehouse	quote €1,800	dispatch	4 days	order	check stock	ship	warehouse

3. ▶66 Now listen and check your answers.

4. ▶66 Listen again and tick (✔) the phrases for *Order and dispatch* that you hear from the Key language section.

> ### Key language for orders and delivery
>
> **Order and dispatch**
> to make an enquiry
> to ask for a quote
> to send an order for some goods
> to invoice a customer
> to check the stock
> to dispatch a shipment
> to track your order (online)
>
> **Transport and delivery**
> We can ship the goods in 24 hours.
> The order was dispatched to you on Friday 26th July.
> The cargo arrived in Hong Kong by container ship.
> We're in a hurry, so I've sent the parcel by courier.
> We send valuable goods by air freight.
> They delivered the shipment by lorry (BrE) / truck (AmE).
> The van was loaded at the warehouse and unloaded at the offices.

62

Orders and delivery 30

Get ready

5 Match each of these pictures (1–6) with one of the sentences in the Key language section.

Pronunciation Schwa /ə/ endings

1 The schwa sound /ə/ is in the same place in all these words. Where is it?

container   courier   director   distributor   inspector   order   retailer   sender   receiver   wholesaler

2 ▶67 **Listen and repeat.**

TASK

6 Work with a partner. You both want to send a large package to a destination in your country. Exchange information about your companies with each other and decide which would be the best to use.

Student A: Look at the details of delivery company Fast Track below.
Student B: Turn to page 84 and read about Logisticam.

Fact File: Fast Track

Customer satisfaction: ★★★★
Discounts: 10% on shipments over €500
Insurance: No
Tracking: Package number is given when order is confirmed.
Delivery method: Road

Guarantee: Half price for one-day delay. Free after that.
Cost: €300
Delivery time: Standard: 3 days
Express delivery: 24 hours from dispatch (+ €100)
Loading/unloading: Price includes loading/unloading cost.

Follow-up

7 Make brief notes, then talk about delivery and distribution in your business. Describe the order process and delivery methods.

Alternative task for pre-work students online

31 Socialising 4

Speak and respond in social situations

1 What do you say in these situations?

1. You arrive ten minutes late for a meeting.
2. You want to know where Bond Street is.
3. You are in a bar. Your guest is going to pay for the drinks, but you want to pay.
4. You want to invite somebody to dinner.
8. You want to buy a train ticket to Paris.
7. You want to know the journey time to the airport.
6. You are at the hotel reception desk. You want to know what time breakfast is.
5. You want to get off a train, but somebody is in your way.
9. You bump into someone at a conference.
10. It's 17:30 on Friday. You're leaving the office.
11. You have a problem with your hire car.
12. You want a receipt for the taxi.
16. You are buying a new pair of shoes.
15. You offer to drive your visitor to the airport.
14. You can't hear what somebody's saying to you.
13. You are at the hotel reception desk. The battery in your phone is dead.

Listening

2 ▶68 Listen and compare your answers.

Socialising 4

3 What do you say in reply?

Listening

4 ▶69 Listen and compare your answers.

32 Success and failure

Talk about business successes and failures

1 Read this text and discuss why you think the products below failed.

> Over a period of about 40 years, marketing expert Robert McMath developed a museum full of over 65,000 examples of successful and failed products. The failures were unsuccessful for several reasons: some of them were just copies of successful products and offered nothing new ('me too' products); they weren't marketed properly; or customers didn't understand them.

- Dr Care: spray-on toothpaste
- Miller Clear Beer: a beer with no colour
- Heinz green ketchup
- Thirsty Dog!: bottled water for pets

Listening

2 ▶70 **Katie Lao started a plant-food business in Toronto, Canada. Listen and put the scenes from her story in the correct order.**

3 Use the pictures above to tell Katie's story.

Key language for business success and failure

Success
It was a great success / a big hit!
The business took off!

Failure
It was a complete failure / a total disaster.
The money ran out.
The business went bust/bankrupt.

Reacting to success
Congratulations!
Great!
Well done!
Amazing!
You deserved it!

Sympathising
Oh dear.
I'm sorry to hear that.
What went wrong?
Better luck next time.

Giving possible reasons
Maybe/Perhaps it didn't have …
It might/could be because …
I think it failed / was a success because …

Get ready

4 Use the Key language to give possible reasons for these events.
1 The business went bankrupt.
2 The new product was a great success.
3 She got a salary increase.
4 He resigned.

5 Use the Key language to react to these statements.
1 I've just got a promotion!
2 I went for the interview, but I didn't get the job.
3 We didn't get the new contract.
4 We're going to sign a new contract!

Pronunciation /s/ and /z/ sounds

1 ▶71 Listen and repeat these words.

/s/	/z/
product**s**	dollar**s**
parent**s**	Katie'**s**
several	de**s**erved
contract**s**	year**s**
sorry	wa**s**

2 Decide if each of these words has the /s/ or the /z/ sound.

chains   congratulations   result   slow   some   soon   supermarket   these   this

3 ▶72 Listen and check, then repeat.

TASK

6 Work with a partner.

Student A: Make notes and give a short talk on the topic below.

Student B: Listen and comment on what you hear, using the Key language.

Then swap roles.

1 Think of a successful idea or product you know about. Make notes in relation to these questions.
  • When did it happen/start?
  • What was it?
  • Who was involved?
  • Why was it a success?
  • What happened as a result?
2 Do the same for something that failed.

33 Meetings 3

Manage a meeting

1. **In your opinion, which three of these duties of a chairperson are the most important?**

   - Keep to the agenda.
   - Start the meeting on time.
   - Make an action plan.
   - Summarise the main points at the end.
   - Make sure the meeting achieves its objectives.
   - Prepare the participants before the meeting begins.
   - Control the meeting.
   - Include everybody in the meeting.

2. **Think of meetings you've attended which didn't achieve their objectives. Why was that?**

Listening

3. **You're going to hear an extract from a staff committee meeting at which these issues are discussed. Before you listen, order the points for the agenda according to their importance.**

   a The finance department has recently received expense claims such as these: a weekend in a hotel for an employee with her husband and children; first-class train tickets; a dry-cleaning bill. The managers who submitted the claims say that nobody told them they couldn't claim for these items.

   b It's extremely difficult to find a space in the company car park. Some employees live very near, but they all come to work by car, because there's no public transport service to the company.

   c Susan Wren, a factory worker, is threatening to take legal action against the foreman, George Blake. She says he has bullied her and other workers for the last four years.

   d Profits at the company were slightly down last year, and there are rumours of big job cuts circulating in the office. Some people are already looking for other jobs.

4. ▶73 **Now listen and compare the order of the meeting agenda with your own from Exercise 3.**

5. ▶73 **Look at the expressions in the Key language section on page 69, then listen again and tick (✔) the ones you hear.**

Key language for leading meetings

Introductions
Good afternoon, ladies and gentlemen. Welcome to …
Does everybody have a copy of the agenda?
Right, shall we start?

Explaining the purpose of the meeting
The reason we're here today is to discuss / consider / decide on / look at …

Prioritising
The first/main point on the agenda is …
Let's start with …

Moving the meeting on
Let's move on to the next point on the agenda.
Let's look at the next point now.

Following up
Let's organise another meeting on 3rd December to check progress / report back on …

Closing the meeting
So, to summarise, …
I think we can finish there for today.

Pronunciation Intonation in questions

1. ▶74 Listen again to the questions from the staff committee meeting, paying attention to the way the speakers' voices go up or down when asking a question, then choose the correct prepositions to complete these rules.
   1. *Wh–* questions usually have an intonation which goes *up / down*.
   2. *Yes/No* questions usually have an intonation which goes *up / down*.

2. Draw arrows to show if the voice rises (↗) or falls (↘) in these questions.
   1. Shall we start?
   2. Does everybody have a copy of the agenda?
   3. Is there any truth in these stories?
   4. What do you suggest we do about Blake?
   5. Any ideas?
   6. What can be claimed on expenses?
   7. Jessica, what do you think?

Get ready

6. Work in small groups. You're going to have a meeting to discuss the agenda in Exercise 3. Study the Key language, decide on a chairperson and begin your meeting. Before you start, look back at the Key language for opinions on page 43.

TASK

7. Agree an agenda of issues in your workplace to discuss with other members of your group. Then hold your meeting.

Alternative task for pre-work students online

34 Our competitors

1 Look at these pieces of advice (1–8) for a business working against a strong competitor. Tick (✔) how good you think each piece is. Explain your choices.

Compare products and services

Analyse your competitors

	Good	Quite good	Bad	It depends
1 Concentrate on your customers, not on your competitors.				
2 Buy examples of your competitors' products or services.				
3 Try to compete for the same markets.				
4 Sell your products at a lower price.				
5 Follow your competitors' customers on social media.				
6 Copy their products.				
7 Understand how your competitors operate.				
8 Make your products different.				

Listening

2 ▶75 Listen to a conversation between a man and woman. The woman would like to buy one of the folding bikes shown in the table below. Which one does she choose?

3 ▶75 Listen again and fill in the missing information in the table.

	City Star	Lux	Cavendish
weight	12kg	18.5kg	1 _____
metal	2 _____	steel	carbon fibre
comfort	4 stars	5 stars	3 stars
wheel diameter	3 _____	40cm	50cm
folding time	6 seconds	10 seconds	4 _____
price	5 _____	$400	$1,200

70

Our competitors 34

Key language for comparing products and services

What's the difference **between** these products?
The size is **the same as** that one.
Our products are very **different from** theirs.
This hotel is near the airport, **while** that one's 20 miles away.

The City Star's **lighter than** the Lux.
The Cavendish is **the lightest**.
The City Star's **more comfortable than** the Cavendish.
The Lux is **the most comfortable**.

Pronunciation The schwa /ə/ in comparative sentences

1 ▶76 **Listen and highlight the schwa /ə/ in these sentences. How many can you find?**
   1 The City Star's lighter than the Lux.
   2 It's better than the bigger one.
   3 This film's older than that one.
   4 The size is the same as the blue bike.

2 ▶76 **Listen again and repeat.**

Get ready

4 **Think of three hotels you know. Make sentences comparing them using the adjectives in the box.**

   bad   cheap   comfortable   expensive   good

   Example: The Regent is cheaper than the Gala.
   The Palace is the most expensive of the three.

5 **Do the same for these things.**
   - Three towns: big, small, polluted, rich, near, attractive, modern
   - Three cars: expensive, cheap, comfortable, fast, ugly, reliable
   - Three countries: hot, cold, big, small, mountainous, flat
   - Three sports: violent, safe, thrilling, tiring, old
   - Three films: interesting, boring, new, enjoyable, exciting

TASK

6 **Use the questions in this table to talk about your main competitors.**

1 Who are they?	2 What are their products/services?
• Who are your competitors? • Are their customers the same as yours?	• What's the difference between your products/services and your competitors'?
3 What are they like?	**4 Better or worse?**
• Are your competitors bigger than you? • How big are they? • Are they growing? Why? • Which competitors are the biggest threat? • Which are the most profitable? Why? • How do your competitors promote themselves?	• In which ways are your competitors stronger than you? • In which ways are they weaker than you?

Alternative task for pre-work students online

35 Our market

Talk about markets and market share

1. The 'sharing economy' is growing fast. Which of these would you share with strangers? Why? / Why not?
   - accommodation
   - a car
   - objects at home, e.g. a camera, a drill

2. The graph below shows the growth of the holiday rental market for four companies between 2011 and 2016. Guess the market share of these platforms on the graph by matching the companies (1–4) with the colours on the graph.

   1 TripAdvisor
   2 HomeAway
   3 Airbnb
   4 Booking.com

   Check your answers on page 102.

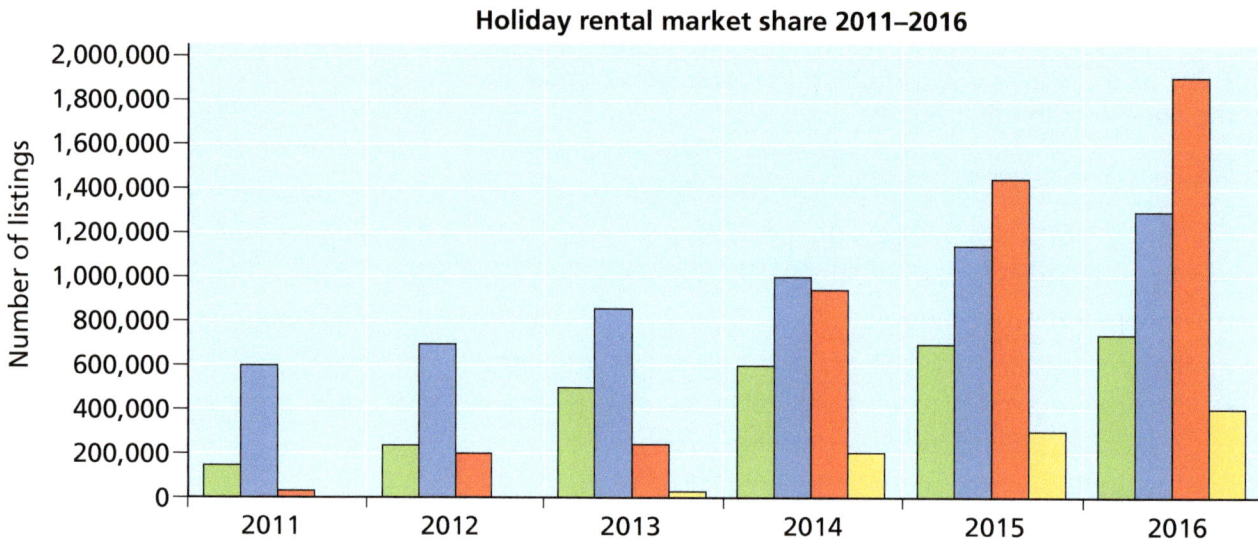

Holiday rental market share 2011–2016

3. Why do you think the holiday rental market has grown so much?

Key language for describing markets	
Proportions	**Movements**
nearly all	The total market is expanding/shrinking.
most people / the majority of people	They increased their market share by 100%.
over half of customers	They doubled their sales.
only a few people	Their share grew by 60%.
… had about a 10% share of the market.	They increased their share a little.
	They lost a lot of their share.
	Sales fell.

Pronunciation Regular past tense endings describing movement

1. Remember that two of the possible sounds for regular past-tense endings are /d/ and /t/. Which sound do these verbs have?

   1 doubl**ed**   3 reach**ed**   5 increas**ed**
   2 compar**ed**   4 chang**ed**   6 decreas**ed**

2. ⏵77 Listen and check, then listen again and repeat.

Our market 35

Get ready

4 Look at the graph in Exercise 2 and use expressions from the Key language section to complete these sentences.

1 In 2011, _____ used Airbnb.
2 In 2011, _____ used HomeAway.
3 In 2013, TripAdvisor had just _____ the number of customers of HomeAway.
4 In 2013, TripAdvisor _____ their sales from the previous year.
5 In 2014, Booking.com _____ a little.
6 The total market _____ .

5 The graph below shows the annual global revenue for car-sharing services between 2014 and 2030. There are three kinds of service:

▪ **Street rental service:** Cars parked on the street are located, used and left (e.g. Zipcar, car2go, DriveNow).

▪ **Ride-sharing, taxis and carpooling:** Private drivers pick up customers using their own vehicles (e.g. Uber, Lyft, BlaBlaCar).

▪ **Robotic car services:** Driverless cars which can be called and used.

What can you say about:
1 the market share of ride-sharing up to now?
2 the future of robotic car services?
3 the total market?

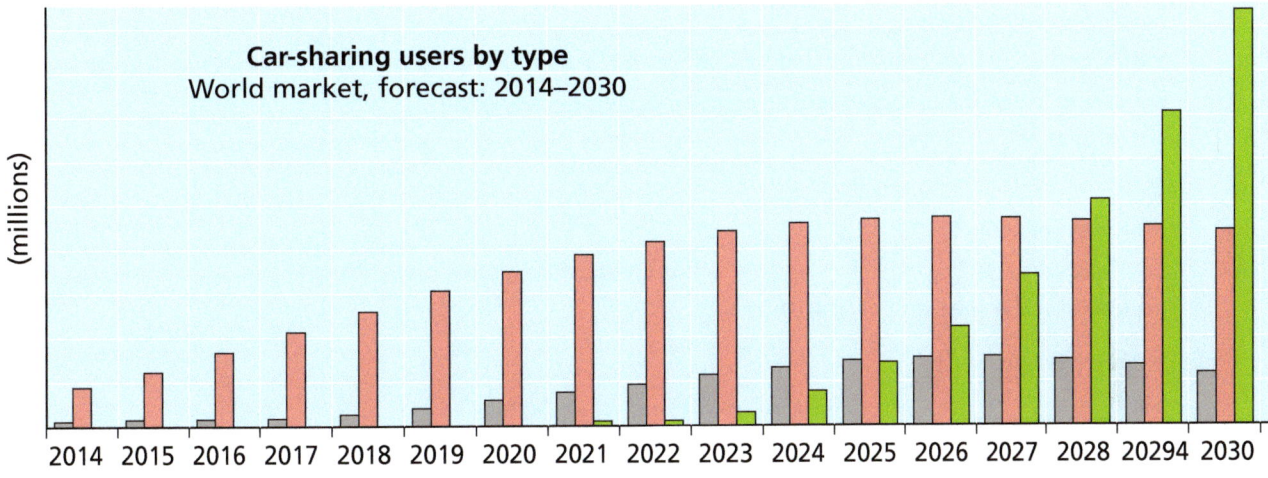

6 Complete the text below about the car-sharing graph using expressions from the box.

| compared to   due to   fall slightly   grow strongly   market leader   overtake |

The total global market for car sharing should continue to ¹_____ . Since the early days, customers have preferred ride-sharing ²_____ street rental services, and the private-driver service is expected to keep its greater share of the market.

However, according to the forecast, both street rental and ride-sharing might start to ³_____ in 2027 ⁴_____ the introduction of robotic car services. While ride-sharing services will continue to be the ⁵_____ till 2028, at this point robotic car services might ⁶_____ them. By 2030, it is expected that most passengers will choose a robot to drive them.

7 ▶78 Listen and check your answers.

TASK

8 Work with a partner. Ask each other and answer about your markets. Use graphics where possible.

- What is your market?
- How big is it?
- Is it a new market?
- Is it expanding or shrinking? Why?
- Is your share of the market growing or falling? Why?

Alternative task for pre-work students online

36 New communications

Talk about communication technology

1 Do you use a smartphone or tablet? Which answer is closest to your opinion?
   a Yes. I have to have the latest version of everything.
   b I've got a smartphone and a laptop, but they're a few years old.
   c I don't feel comfortable with technology. I have a smartphone, but I avoid using it if possible.

2 What kind of communication technology do you think you'll have in ten years' time?

Listening

3 ▶79 Listen to two people talking about the advantages and disadvantages of using different types of communication technology and complete these notes.

> Internal communication
> - Easier for companies to ¹_____ .
> - Staff can ²_____ with the office.
> - E-mailing, instant messaging and connecting to social networking encourages ³_____ .
>
> but
> - Too many internal ⁴_____ .
> - Employees always ⁵_____ . This creates tiring conditions, leading to low morale and poor productivity.
>
> Improved productivity
> - Many ⁶_____ — e.g. maps, calendars, contact lists — instantly available.
> - ⁷_____ with your office anywhere in the world.
>
> but
> - Lots of distractions.
> - You can produce absolutely nothing of value!
>
> Customer service
> - Don't ⁸_____ visiting customers.
> - Access customers' sites/servers ⁹_____
>
> but
> - Security — is our data ¹⁰_____ ?

Pronunciation Weak form of *can*

▶80 In fast spoken English, the word *can* is pronounced /kən/. Listen to these examples and practise saying them.
1 Staff can always check their e-mails.
2 This can lead to low morale.
3 New technology can really improve productivity.
4 I can access their servers remotely.

New communications 36

Key language for describing communication devices

I have a smartphone/laptop/notebook/tablet.

It's
- state-of-the-art / the latest edition / cutting edge.
- not very new.
- obsolete.
- small / compact / very light.
- bulky/heavy.

Its processing power is super-fast / a bit sluggish / dead slow.
It has 256 GB (gigabytes) of memory.
You can upgrade the memory / processor / operating system.

The battery life is
- great. It lasts all day.
- terrible. I have to recharge it every day.

It has
- Bluetooth.
- two USB ports.
- a micro SD card slot / HDMI output.
- wi-fi.

Get ready

4 Match these products (a–c) with the descriptions (1–3).

smartphone

tablet

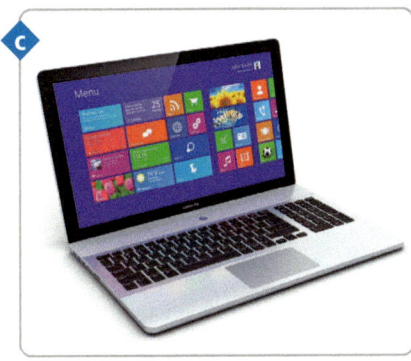
laptop

1 It's convenient and light-weight. I use it to present our products, facts and figures with interactive audio-visual apps. I can link it to the devices of people I'm presenting to, but it doesn't have the power and functions of a PC.

2 I only use this when I'm working from home or in the office, to catch up with admin or preparing for meetings and presentations. It's a bit bulky and heavy to carry around.

3 It keeps me in touch with the office, clients and other colleagues through calls and e-mails. I can also use it as a sat-nav. You need a good signal or a wi-fi connection, otherwise it can be frustrating.

TASK

5 Prepare to talk about the types of communication technology you use in your job. What do you think are the main advantages and disadvantages of using these in your business?

Follow-up

6 Are you loyal to a particular brand of technological equipment? What do you like about it? What don't you like about other brands?

Alternative task for pre-work students online

37 Import–export

Discuss importing and exporting

Talk about quantity

1 Work with a partner. Match each country (1–10) with its main export (a–j).

Example: **A:** Which country exports the most oil?
B: I think it's Saudi Arabia.

1	Canada	a	oil
2	China	b	gas
3	Italy	c	gold
4	Japan	d	rice
5	Russia	e	fish
6	Saudi Arabia	f	cars
7	South Africa	g	agricultural produce
8	South Korea	h	electronic goods
9	Thailand	i	wine
10	US	j	ships

2 What are your country's main imports and exports?

3 Who are your country's most important trading partners?

Pronunciation Word stress in countries and nationalities

1 ▶81 How do you pronounce these countries and nationalities? Underline where you think the stressed syllable is. Then listen and check.

1	Japan	Japanese	4	Vietnam	Vietnamese
2	Italy	Italian	5	Europe	European
3	China	Chinese	6	Egypt	Egyptian

2 ▶81 Listen again and repeat.

Key language for quantity

Countable nouns
How many cars does Japan export?
It exports **a lot / lots** of cars.
How many ships does South Korea import?
It imports **a few** ships.

Uncountable nouns
How much gold does South Africa export?
It exports **a lot / lots** of gold.
How much wine does Italy import?
It imports **a little** wine.

Import–export 37

4 Ask and answer questions about the photos using *How much* and *How many*.

Example: 1
A: How much gas is there?
B: There's a lot.

1. gas
2. euros
3. plastic
4. water
5. diamonds
6. oil
7. money
8. rice
9. silver
10. time

TASK

5 Jim Fletcher began his own import–export company six years ago in Vancouver, Canada. Here, he's talking about the experience of starting his own business and a typical day at work. Work with a partner to complete the missing information in your texts.

Student A: Look at this page.
Student B: Turn to page 87.

Student A

Starting an import–export business

❝ If you plan to work from home, you only need about (*How much?*) $_____ to start your own import–export business. If you plan to open an office, then it'll cost at least $25,000. You'll have to pay rent, hire employees, etc.

At the start, you should focus on (*How many?*) _____ products, those which you know will sell well. There are a lot of regulations in this business, so you need to find out about them. For example, a few products, like (*Which?*) _____ , need special licences. ❞

A typical day

❝ I spend (*How long?*) _____ in the office and the rest of time I travel. If I'm in the office, the first thing I do in the morning is make some coffee and talk to my assistant. Then I check my (*What?*) _____ and answer the phone. We get lots of calls from foreign companies about (*What?*) _____ – things like that. Then I usually make a few calls to check the progress of orders. I also talk with (*Who?*) _____ on Skype once or twice a day.

The afternoon is usually a bit quieter. I work on contracts and do a little research (*Why?*) _____ . I try to finish work at six o'clock, but sometimes that's not possible if there are problems. ❞

Follow-up

6 Discuss these questions.
- Does your business use imported goods? Why?
- Does your company export? How much? Where?
- What can be some of the problems with importing goods?
- What can be some of the problems with exporting goods?
- Would you like to work in the import–export business? Why?

Alternative task for pre-work students online

38 Socialising 5

Talk about behaviour when doing business internationally

1. In 2013, Bill Gates met the South Korean President, Park Geun-hye. Do you think they greeted each other appropriately? Why? / Why not?

Key language for discussing business etiquette

Giving advice	Actions
You need to find out about the culture of the country.	to shake hands
It's not a good idea to ask about your host's family / discuss politics, etc.	to bow
It's polite to …	to greet guests
It's considered rude to …	to introduce people
It's considered insulting to …	to offer your business card
	to make (hand) gestures
	to allow personal space
	to behave appropriately
	to dress appropriately/formally/casually
	to be too direct/indirect
	to be too informal/formal
	to invite people to lunch
	body language

TASK

2. Work with a partner. Describe what's happening in pictures 1–15. What's the problem in each case? You can check your answers on page 102.

Is Stockholm the capital of Denmark?

3 Which of the situations apply to your own culture?

39 The economy

Describe economic trends

1 **Choose the options that are true in sentences 1 and 2 and complete sentences 3 and 4.**
  1 At the moment, my country's economy is performing *very well / well / quite well / badly / very badly*.
  2 The main reasons for this are *high / low* production in *industry / services / agriculture* and *strong / weak* exports.
  3 Other reasons for this are …
  4 The strongest economies in the world at the moment are …

Listening

2 ▶82 **Listen to a description of the economy of New Zealand. Is it generally positive or negative?**

3 ▶82 **Listen again and choose the best answers.**
  1 The economy is mainly *industrial / agricultural*.
  2 New Zealand manufactures *machinery / cars*.
  3 More than *22 million / 2 million* tourists visit annually.
  4 The economy is *growing / shrinking*.
  5 Unemployment is at *5.4% / 4.5%*.
  6 New Zealand has a *higher / lower* tax rate than Chile.

Get ready

4 **Match these photos with words from the Key language section on page 81.**

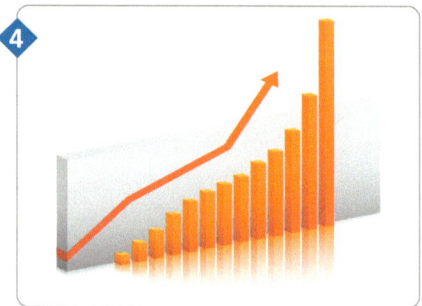  

5 Match the sentence halves.

1 The economy
2 Unemployment is
3 There is a
4 The exchange rate is $1.32
5 The national debt is high. We owe
6 Property prices
7 The income tax
8 The main public spending is on education,
9 Energy sources are gas, oil,

a are falling.
b at 7%.
c billions of dollars.
d boom/recession.
e health and transport.
f is growing.
g nuclear and renewables.
h rate is 18%.
i to the euro.

Key language for talking about the economy

agricultural
industrial   } sector
manufacturing

service
inflation
unemployment

GDP (Gross Domestic Product: the total value of all goods and services produced in a country in a year)
a boom/recession
currency
national debt
property prices
taxation / tax rates
public spending
energy: gas, oil, nuclear, renewables

Pronunciation Stress in word families

1 ▶83 **The stressed syllable changes in these word families. Listen and underline the main stressed syllable that you hear.**

1 economy   economics   economical
2 industry   industrial
3 agriculture   agricultural
4 manufacture   manufacturing

2 ▶83 **Listen again and repeat.**

TASK

6 You're going to give a short presentation about part of your economy. Choose three or four of these points and prepare your talk.

- the economy (agricultural, industrial, service sectors)
- manufacturing
- economic growth
- energy
- inflation
- unemployment
- GDP
- currency
- national debt
- property prices
- public spending
- taxation

40 International business quiz

Divide into two teams (A and B).

Team A: Ask Team B the questions in this quiz. The answers are on page 87.
Do not look at page 83.

Team A

1 You are at an international conference. What do these sentences mean?

   a *Please have a seat.*

   b *Can I give you a lift?*

2 Who was the business leader shown on your page?

3 What is the trend called from national economic units to one big global market?

4 True or false? If you have a *hotline*, it means the work must be finished by that date.

5 Look at the e-mail address on your page. Spell it out loud.

6 True or false? *CIF* is a term used in international trade, which means that the seller pays the cost of transport to the ship, insurance and freight to the destination port.

7 Which of these is widely considered to be the biggest-selling toy of all time: PlayStation or Rubik's Cube?

8 Name one of the international ports shown on your page.

9 What did Nils Bohlin of Volvo invent in 1959?

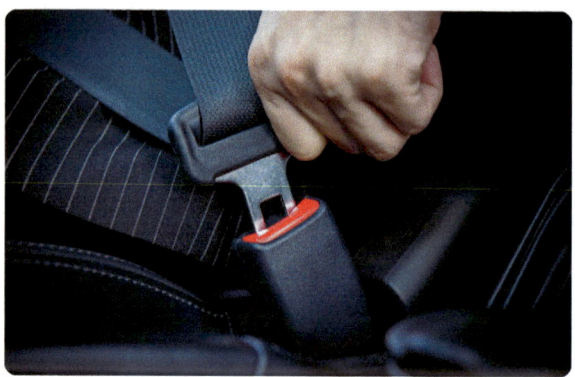

10 Which of these countries is home to the world's largest seaport?

   a the US
   b the Netherlands
   c China

11 Where is the headquarters of the World Trade Organisation?

12 Which of these companies had the highest revenues in the world in 2017?

   a Walmart
   b Royal Dutch Shell
   c ING Group

13 In 2018, how many countries were using the euro as their currency?

   a 14   b 19   c 23

14 Which countries have these internet suffixes?

   a de   b th   c au

5

International business quiz 40

Team B: Ask Team A the questions in this quiz. The answers are on page 88.
Do not look at page 82.

Team B

1 What are the five BRICS countries that are becoming major forces in the world's economy?

2 True or false? Motorola was the first company to produce a mobile phone.

3 You are at an international conference. What do these sentences mean?

   a Can I get back to you on that?

   b I'll give you a ring.

4 Who invented the safety razor in 1895?
5 Who is the business leader shown on your page?
6 In which of these countries would you drive on the left?
   a Thailand   b Japan   c Australia

7 True or false? *Free on board (FOB)* is a term used in international trade which means the seller pays only the cost of transport to the ship and insurance. The freight charges are paid by the buyer.

8 What does *GDP* stand for?
9 What were the three top exporting countries in 2017?
10 What is the *ASEAN*?
11 Ships carry cargo internationally in large metal boxes. What are these boxes called?
12 Which countries use these currencies?
   a rupee   b krone   c baht
13 You're landing at Schiphol Airport. Which city are you near?

14 Which of these countries is in the EU?
   a Switzerland
   b Norway
   c Iceland

2

5 silic.josip@freenet.ca

8

Activity files

Unit 4, Exercise 6

Student B

Student A is going to call you to arrange a meeting.

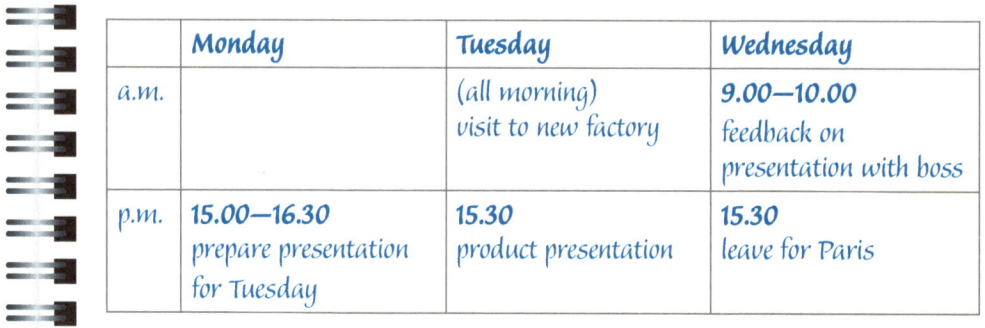

	Monday	Tuesday	Wednesday
a.m.		(all morning) visit to new factory	9.00–10.00 feedback on presentation with boss
p.m.	15.00–16.30 prepare presentation for Tuesday	15.30 product presentation	15.30 leave for Paris

Unit 6, Exercise 6

QUESTIONNAIRE SCORES

20–32 points
It seems you need to improve your soft skills. Look at where you lost points. Maybe you should try to show more initiative at work, volunteer for difficult jobs, promote yourself a little more and improve your participation in meetings and presentations.

33–46 points
Your soft skills are not bad, but they could be better. Look at where you lost points. Perhaps you should try to improve your relationship with your colleagues, express yourself more and be more positive.

47–60 points
Congratulations! Your soft skills look good – but you're not perfect! Check the areas where you lost points. How could you improve?

Unit 30, Exercise 6

Student B

Fact File: Logisticam

Customer satisfaction: ★★★★★
Discounts: 10% on shipments over €200
Insurance: Price includes insurance
Tracking: By phone enquiry
Delivery method: Road

Guarantee: No
Cost: €250
Delivery time: 4–5 days
Loading/unloading: Price doesn't include loading/unloading cost.

Unit 7, Exercise 4

Student B

You don't need to give any of the detailed company information yet, you'll use that in Unit 8. For now, just:

- introduce yourself
- present the subject
- refer to timing and questions
- describe the presentation structure
- give the opening lines of your presentation.

Instagram

Background
- A photo- and video-sharing social networking service
- Bought by Facebook in 2012 for $1 billion
- Popular with users who want to see images rather than text

Users
- Total number of daily active Instagram users (2017): 500 million
- 68% of Instagram users are females
- Most users are between 18 and 29 years old
- 25 million business profiles using Instagram (2018)

Finance
- Revenue (2017): $3.64 billion
- Revenue more than doubled each year between 2014 and 2017

Unit 21, Exercise 5

Student B

JK Hardware   23 Blackstone Road   Blackstone   East Sussex BT6 8KD   Tel. 01273 55983

Carlton Plc
48 Thames Street
London W1D 1LA

Invoice no. 634

Account no.	Invoice date:
BRN877	22/11/19

Product code	Description	Quantity	Unit price	Total
PD15486	F23 tablet computer	45	£387.42	£17,433.90
KJ50	X90 back-up drive	37	£59.90	£2,216.30
Subtotal				£19,650.20
Less 10% discount				£1,865.02
Total due				**£17,785.18**

Activity files

Unit 22, Exercise 4

Student B

Unit 22, Exercise 5

Student B

Use the Key language on page 46 to describe the movements on this graph to Student A. It shows historical changes in the price of silver in the UK.

Unit 29, Exercise 7

Student B

Describe how pear brandy is made.

- a bottle | put over a baby pear and the bottle | tie to the branch

- it | take down when the pear has grown
- the bottle and pear | wash by hand
- the bottle | fill with brandy

Unit 37, Exercise 5

Student B

Starting an import–export business

❝ If you plan to work from home, you only need about $8,000 to start your own import–export business. If you plan to open an office, then it'll cost at least (*How much?*) $_____. You'll have to pay rent, hire employees, etc.

At the start, you should focus on a few products, those which you know will sell well. There are (*How many?*) _____ regulations in this business, so you need to find out about them. For example, a few products, like pharmaceuticals, need (*What?*) _____. ❞

A typical day

❝ I spend three or four days a week in the office and the rest of time I travel. If I'm in the office, the first thing I do in the morning is (*What?*) _____ and talk to my assistant. Then I check my e-mails and answer the phone. We get (*How many?*) _____ calls from foreign companies about prices, quantities, dates – things like that. Then I usually make (*How many?*) _____ calls to check the progress of orders. I also talk with my partners on Skype (*How often?*) _____.

The afternoon is usually a bit quieter. I work on contracts and do a little research to find new business. I try to finish work at (*What time?*) _____, but sometimes that's not possible if there are problems. ❞

Unit 40 Team A

1. **a** Sit down.
   b Would you like to travel with me?
2. Henry Ford (1863–1947), founder of the Ford Motor Company
3. Globalisation
4. False. That's a *deadline*. A hotline is phone number that gives you direct access to someone important or for use in emergencies.
5. s-i-l-i-c dot j-o-s-i-p at freenet dot c-a
6. True
7. Rubik's Cube
8. **a** Shanghai **b** Los Angeles
9. Car seatbelts
10. c (Shanghai)
11. Geneva, Switzerland
12. a (Walmart's revenue in 2017 was $500 billion)
13. b
14. **a** Germany **b** Thailand **c** Australia

Activity files

Unit 40 Team B

1 Brazil, Russia, India, China, South Africa
2 True
3 a I can't answer that at the moment. Can I talk to you about it later?
  b I'll call you by phone.
4 King C. Gillette
5 Richard Branson (1950–), founder of the Virgin Group
6 All of them
7 True
8 Gross Domestic Product
9 1 China ($2,263 billion)
  2 USA ($1,546 billion)
  3 Germany ($1,448 billion)
  (Source: www.statista.com)
10 Association of South-East Asian Nations
11 Containers
12 a India   b Denmark, Sweden, Norway   c Thailand
13 Amsterdam (in the Netherlands)
14 None of them

Audio scripts

Audio 01
Interviewer: Who do you work for?
Man: I work for Jonson Foods Limited.
Interviewer: Is that J-O-H-...
Man: No, J-O-N-S-O-N.
Interviewer: Thanks. And what do you do?
Man: I'm a Quality Inspector.
Interviewer: So you work in the Quality Department.
Man: In the Quality Control Department, yes. I usually work in the laboratory.
Interviewer: Right. And where are you based?
Man: I'm based at the company's plant in Newcastle.
Interviewer: Do you work full-time or part-time?
Man: Full-time. I'd prefer to work part-time actually, but I can't, so it's nine to five, five days a week.
Interviewer: And who do you report to at work?
Man: My boss is Susan Hill – she's the Quality Control Manager.
Interviewer: So what would you say is the main purpose of your job?
Man: The main thing I have to do is to make sure our raw materials and finished products meet the company standards. I usually work on our cheese products.
Interviewer: Cheese?
Man: Yes.
Interviewer: Do you have any other responsibilities?
Man: Er, yes. I have to inspect the quality of the packaging as well. Last week, for example, we couldn't open some of the plastic wrappers on the cheese slices very easily and so I had to ...

Audio 02
1 Where do you work?
2 Who do you work for?
3 What do you do?
4 What time do you leave work?
5 Where are you based?
6 Who do you report to at work?
7 What would you say is the main purpose of your job?
8 When do you take your holidays?
9 What time do you have a break?

Audio 03
Interviewer: Who do you communicate with in your company, Alice?
Alice: Well, inside the company, I suppose I communicate most with my colleagues in the Art Department.
Interviewer: And what do you talk to them about?
Alice: It depends on what stage we're at in a project, but it's usually about design.
Interviewer: Who else do you talk to?
Alice: I speak to my boss, of course – then personnel from other departments, sometimes in meetings, sometimes in their offices. I talk to the Finance Manager a lot. Especially this week!
Interviewer: Is there a problem?
Alice: No, not really ... we just think our budget is too small and he doesn't want to give us any more money. He thinks we spend too much. So we argue about that sometimes.
Interviewer: What about external contacts, people outside the company? How often do you speak to them?
Alice: Not every day, but quite often. We have several suppliers who work for us on a project basis, and they often come in to discuss their work.
Interviewer: What about clients or customers?
Alice: Yes, when we produce videos specifically for one client, I certainly have to keep in close contact with them. That can be difficult.
Interviewer: Why?
Alice: Well, one client we have at the moment, for example, is never satisfied. He's always trying to find something wrong – even very small, insignificant details.
Interviewer: What about the media? Do you speak to them?
Alice: No, that's not my job. I leave that to Public Relations.

Audio 04
1 What do you talk to them about?
2 I speak to my boss.
3 Who else do you talk to?
4 I talk to the Finance Manager.
5 We think our budget is too small.
6 He doesn't want to give us any money.
7 He thinks we spend too much.
8 How often do you speak to them?

Audio 05
Man: Hello, Peter Jacobsen's office.
Woman: Oh, hello. It's Pilar Rivera from Mapcorp here. Could I speak to Peter?
Man: I'm sorry, he's away until tomorrow. Have you tried his mobile?
Woman: Yes, but he isn't answering. Could I leave a message with you?
Man: Yes, sure.
Woman: Could you ask him to call me as soon as possible? He's got my number. It's about the meeting on Monday.
Man: Yes, of course, I'll tell him. Was there anything else?
Woman: No, that's all, thanks. Bye.
Man: Goodbye.

Audio 06
1
Carlo: Carlo Ramirez speaking.
Kirsten: Hello, Carlo. It's Kirsten from CTD here.
Carlo: Oh hi, Kirsten.
Kirsten: We've got a problem with your last delivery. The reference number is 180-G-7.
Carlo: OK, I'll need to check that. Can I ask someone to call you back in a minute?
Kirsten: Yes, sure. They can call me direct on 098-63-263.
Carlo: OK, I've got that. Bye.
Kirsten: Bye.

2
Man: Mike Brennan.
Woman: Hello, it's Mrs Barton here. Is my husband there?
Man: I'm sorry, Mrs Barton. He's out with a client.
Woman: Out with a client? Well, he's supposed to be picking our daughter up from school. She's still there waiting for him! I can't go because the only way to get there is by bus, but they're on strike today. That leaves a taxi, but it's impossible to find a taxi because of the strike. Why doesn't he turn his mobile on?! He's just spent a fortune on a new phone and he never switches the thing on it drives me absolutely mad ...

Audio 07
on Friday.
the meeting on Friday.
I'm calling about the meeting on Friday.

at the moment.
he's not in at the moment.
I'm sorry, he's not in at the moment.

a message?
leave a message?
Would you like to leave a message?
back?

89

Audio scripts

call me back?
ask her to call me back?
Could you ask her to call me back?

Audio 08
Alex: Hello.
Sue: Hello, could I speak to Alex Pond, please?
Alex: Speaking.
Sue: It's Sue Jafari from Camco here.
Alex: Hello, Sue, what can I do for you?
Sue: I'm calling about the P3 project.
Alex: Yes, of course.
Sue: We should really arrange a meeting here soon.
Alex: Yes, I agree. This week's not good for me, though – I'm leaving for Warsaw tomorrow. How about next week?
Sue: Yes, I think so. I'll just check my diary. Are you free on Tuesday?
Alex: No, sorry, I'm busy all day on Tuesday. What about Wednesday?
Sue: Wednesday afternoon?
Alex: Yes, that looks OK. Would three o'clock suit you?
Sue: Yes, three o'clock's fine.
Alex: Good. OK, see you on Wednesday at three.
Sue: OK, bye.

Audio 09
1
Alessia: Hello, I'm Alessia. I'm the Quality Control Manager.
Carl: Hello, Alessia. I'm Carl.
Alessia: Nice to meet you.
Carl: You too.
Alessia: Just follow me, please. This is the meeting room. Please have a seat. Would you like a coffee or tea?
Carl: Just some water, please.
Alessia: Sure. Sparkling or still?
Carl: Still, please.
Alessia: OK, I'll just get some. I won't be long …

2
Alessia: Carl, this is Peter. He's the engineer on this project.
Peter: Pleased to meet you, Carl. This is Karen. She's in charge of the finances.
Carl: How do you do?
Karen: How do you do?
Peter: So, did you have a good trip?
Carl: Yes, fine. No problems. There was a slight delay at the airport, but nothing really.
Karen: And is your hotel OK?
Carl: Yes. It's very comfortable, thanks.
Karen: Good. Well, shall we start?
Carl: Yes, fine.
Peter: Right, I think we've all got copies of the agenda, so let's make a start …

3
Carl: It's late. I really must go.
Karen: All right. Can I give you a lift to the airport?
Carl: No, thanks, Karen, I'll get a taxi. I have to go back to the hotel first.
Peter: Well, it was very nice meeting you.
Carl: Thanks, you too. I look forward to seeing you again in July, at the conference.
Karen: Yes, have a good trip. Bye!
Carl: Goodbye!

Audio 10
1. **A:** Pleased to meet you!
   B: Pleased to meet you too!
2. **A:** Would you like a coffee or tea?
   B: A coffee, please!
3. **A:** Did you have a good trip?
   B: Not really. What about you?
4. **A:** How was your flight?
   B: Not too bad, thanks.
5. **A:** It was nice meeting you!
   B: Thanks, you too!

Audio 11
/z/ easy   /s/ sorry   /ð/ they   /θ/ think

Audio 12
/z/ organised, languages, please, presentation
/s/ some, progressing, say, soft, sale, speak, face
/ð/ then, other, their, with
/θ/ thing, thin

Audio 13
Kato: Good afternoon. I'm Kato Lowit and I'm the CEO of G-Frontier, a company which explores and develops the possibilities of that amazing material – graphene. My aim today is to show you our latest and most exciting product and to invite you to invest $450,000 to help in its development. I know that some of you are not engineers, so if I get too technical, please feel free to interrupt. Now, I've divided my presentation into three parts. First of all, I'll explain what the product is exactly; then we'll look at its clear commercial potential; and finally, I'd like to tell you why this investment is so important to us and how you will be able to profit from it. Let's begin by looking at the material itself. What is graphene?

Audio 14
1. You won't be able to access the program without a valid password.
2. After that, I'd like to talk about our sales figures.
3. Don't worry, you can ask questions at the end.
4. Before going on to my next point, let's consider the figures.
5. If you're happy with that, we can move on.
6. As you can see, I've highlighted three main points.
7. Finally, we'll look at the results and come to our conclusions.
8. I work in the sales department and I'm in charge of marketing, too.

Audio 15
Kato: So, first of all, let me explain what the product is exactly. As you can see, it's a filter, and when the sea water passes through it, the salt is blocked. The reason for this is that new graphene filters have holes that are so small that they only allow the tiny water molecules to …
   Let's move on to look at why this product will be a success. Current technology for producing fresh water from sea water involves a very long and expensive process, compared to what we're offering here. Look at this chart comparing production time and costs for standard production techniques …
   Now we come to the reasons why your investment is so important at this stage. Our business plan has reached the point where we need to invest in marketing and promotion, and in order to do this, we need to …
   To sum up, then, what we're offering you is a product which guarantees success and is sure to give you a great return on your investment. Finally, if you have any doubts about the quality of the water produced from our filter, then take another sip of water from the bottles in front of you, because that's it! Thank you.

Audio 16
We're offering a new product.
What does that mean for us?

Audio 17
1. They're‿out.
2. Your‿investment is important.
3. Their‿office is in Singapore.
4. You're‿older than me.
5. Where‿are they?
6. There‿isn't much time.

Audio 18
Sachitar: Well, let's start with sleep. I go to bed at 11 nearly every night and I usually get up at seven. Then I leave the house after an hour, at eight o'clock, and in the evening I get home at seven, if I'm lucky. So personal time is one hour in the morning plus another four hours in the evening. Travelling next: it takes me two hours to get to work with all the traffic and an hour to get back home. Then, work: I spend a long time sitting in meetings – meetings with sales, planning meetings, meetings with media agencies, management meetings … I probably spend at least four hours a day in meetings. Far too much! A lot of the meetings are a waste of time!
   I spend the rest of the time at work on my computer, analysing data and writing e-mails, or on the phone. In fact, this is often my most important work, but I haven't got enough time to do it. I don't really have much time for lunch, it's usually just half an hour in the company restaurant. I try to have two breaks a day, maybe 15 minutes each.

Audio 19
1 debt   date
2 gate   get
3 we'll will
4 its   eats
5 bin   been
6 west   waste
7 sleep slept
8 this   these

Audio 20
Greta Paget: Our interview procedure depends on the position we're interviewing for, but there are generally four main stages.

First of all, we arrange a face-to-face interview or a phone interview. The candidate might be hundreds of kilometres away or even in another country, so we use either the phone or Skype. During this first interview, we usually ask the candidate detailed questions about their work experience.

Then, if we call the candidate for a second interview, they're doing well. At that point, they'll meet the person they'll report to in the organisation – their future boss – often the head of the department. This is more like a conversation between two professionals than an interview. The department head will tell the candidate about the responsibilities of the job and try to find out if they have the necessary skills to deal with these responsibilities. After that, they'll hear more about the salary.

Now, if they pass the second interview, well, they've arrived! The third interview is with Human Resources and the Finance Department. They'll discuss contracts and salary with the candidate.

And finally, after waiting a few days, the successful candidate will receive written confirmation from the department head and a job offer.

Audio 21
1 First of all, we arrange a face-to-face interview.
2 So we use either the phone or Skype.
3 Then if we call the candidate for a second interview, they're doing well.
4 After that, they'll hear more about the salary.
5 And finally, the successful candidate will receive a job offer.

Audio 22
Interviewer: Good morning! On today's show, we're talking to stress counsellor Angela Polinski, whose book *Stress: Make it work for you* is a bestseller. Angela, firstly, congratulations on your book! Why do you think it's so successful?
Angela: Hi there! Well, probably because it touches on three main areas, which affect most people at some time in their lives.
Interviewer: And they are …?
Angela: Work … things like performance evaluations, lazy colleagues, long working hours. Then there's money – stuff such as unexpected bills, education costs, job uncertainty. Probably the most stressful areas of our lives, though, are in our relationships with others – things like divorce or separation, difficult teenagers, noisy neighbours and so on.
Interviewer: So what can happen as a result of this stress?
Angela: The consequences can be serious. For one thing, you can develop health problems due to stress, so people should really think more about it.
Interviewer: But what can we do? Is there always an answer?
Angela: Yes, I think so. It's a question of managing your life better. For example, if you feel under too much pressure because of work targets or deadlines, you need to look at your schedule and prioritise the most important things. If it's your rent or your mortgage repayments, then talk to your bank and try to rearrange your finances. If your kids stress you out because you don't spend enough time with them, then rearrange your schedule. You won't be sorry!

Audio 23
talk   would   Wednesday
psychologist   resign   doubt
straight   listen   mortgage

Audio 24
Woman: 'Fried sea bass'. What does that mean?
Man: Sea bass is a kind of fish, and fried means it's cooked in hot oil.
Woman: And what about 'Asparagus and leek'?
Man: Asparagus is a long, green vegetable. Leeks are long as well, but they're white at the bottom.
Woman: Oh, yes. OK.
Waiter: Good evening, are you ready to order?
Woman: Yes, I think so.
Man: Yes. I'd like the asparagus and leek soup to start, please.
Waiter: Certainly.
Woman: And I'll have the same.
Waiter: Two asparagus and leek soup. And for the main course?
Man: Grilled chicken for me, and could I have potatoes with that?
Waiter: Of course. Mashed potatoes or chips or …?
Man: Chips will be fine.
Waiter: Right, and for you, madam?
Woman: What do you recommend?
Waiter: Well, the baked red pepper is always a favourite with our regular customers.
Woman: OK. Does it come with rice?
Waiter: You can have rice with that. Fried or steamed?
Woman: Er, no … I've changed my mind. I'll have the fried sea bass instead.
Waiter: OK, one sea bass … Would you like to order the dessert now or later?
Woman: Later, please.
Man: Yes, later.
Waiter: Fine, and to drink?
Man: Some mineral water.
Waiter: Still or sparkling?
Woman: Sparkling, please. A litre.
Waiter: One litre. Would you like to see the wine list?
Man: Yes, please.
Waiter: I'll bring it straight away.

Audio 25
baked, cake, change, grape, main, same, straight, waiter
buy, fried, I'll, rice, right, wine
grow, know, show, smoked
now, our, shower, sound
beer, hear, near

Audio 26
Man 1: OK, we all know why we're here.
Woman 1: Yes. Dad refuses to create a company website and start selling online.
Man 2: He doesn't understand that we're living in a different world now. The shop's not enough. We have to sell on the internet, too.
Woman 2: Why doesn't your dad want to?
Woman 1: Because of the cost. He says it's too expensive.
Man 1: So what can we do?
Man 2: I think he should just retire. He's 63 now!
Woman 1: Look, you know he isn't ready to retire yet. He wants to carry on for a few years.
Man 1: I don't think he should retire either, and not only for personal reasons. With his experience, Dad's very useful to the business in lots of ways.
Man 2: Well, in that case, we'll just have to persuade him to accept that we are going to start selling online.
Man 1: But how?
Woman 1: I know – how about showing him some really good retail sites on the web and how user-friendly they are? Then maybe he'll begin to see that—
Man 1: No, he won't. He'll just say, 'Oh yes, very nice, but far too expensive. We can't afford luxuries like that.' You know what he's like.
Woman 1: Margaret, what do you think?
Woman 2: Well, I was dealing with another retail company's accounts the other day. They started using a website two years ago, and the positive effect of it on their sales is very clear from the accounts. So I suggest showing these figures to your dad. Show him a fact, a real example of the difference a website can make to sales. He can't argue with that!

Audio scripts

Woman 1: Yes, that's it, Margaret.
Man 1: Yeah – good idea.

Audio 27
Their father didn't want to set up a website because of the cost.
As the cost was high, their father didn't want to set up a website.

Audio 28
As we often don't have the goods in stock, there are delivery delays to customers.
Our computer system is very slow because it's ten years old.
I missed the train, so I was late for the meeting.
We're spending too much because of the high price of the dollar.

Audio 29
1 Do I have to change trains?
2 How much luggage do you have?

Audio 30
1 I have to go.
2 Have you got your passport?
3 I've got two suitcases.
4 You have to hurry.
5 Do you know which train I have to get?
6 I haven't got a boarding card.

Audio 31
1 Hello, I'd like some information about flights to Los Angeles.
2 Could you tell me what time Flight LA562 arrives?
3 Can you tell me how to get to Gatwick Airport?
4 Could you tell me which terminal flight LA562 leaves from?
5 Excuse me. I want to go to Victoria. Do you know which train I have to take?
6 Do I have to change trains?
7 Can you tell me what time the next train to Gatwick is?
8 How long does it take to get there?
9 How much is a single ticket to Gatwick?
10 I've got two suitcases and one piece of hand luggage.
11 A window seat, please.
12 Excuse me. Do you know where Gate 32 is?

Audio 32
Where did you go to school?
I've got a degree in Modern Languages from Bologna University.
I worked for a company in Milan for two years.

Audio 33
1 I'm going to look for a new job.
2 She comes from Berlin.
3 I went to school in France.
4 Are you going to stay in this job for long?

Audio 34
Man: Elisa, where and when were you born?
Woman: I was born in Elstree, UK, on the 4th of April, 1995.
Man: Where do you live?
Woman: I live in Milan.
Man: OK. Where did you go to school?
Woman: I went to Hawksmoor School in Watford.
Man: Did you go to university?
Woman: Yes, I went to university in Bologna.
Man: What qualifications do you have?
Woman: I've got a Bachelor's degree in Modern Languages.
Man: What work experience do you have?
Woman: Well, after university, I started work in a logistics company as an assistant to the European manager. Then I left that job and I —
Man: Why did you leave that job?
Woman: Oh, I left because I wanted to find a position with more responsibility. There weren't any possibilities of promotion in that company.
Man: Did you find another job?
Woman: Yes, I now work as Logistics Co-ordinator for ITC Trading in Milan.
Man: Are you going to stay in this job for long?
Woman: I like the work, but I'm going to look for a position as Logistics Manager next year.
Man: How long have you been in this job?
Woman: For two years.

Audio 35
1 Pierre Omidyar started the company in San José, USA, in September 1995. He wanted to provide a marketplace for the sale of goods and services to people. Their website now gets several million views daily. How do they make a profit? When an item is listed on the website, the seller must pay a small charge. Then, at the end of the auction, there is another charge of between 1.25 and 5% of the sale price.
2 The company was founded on the 5th of February, 1890, by Carl von Thieme and Wilhelm von Finck. It opened a branch office in London a few years later. Now it's one of the biggest players in the world of financial services and, in particular, insurance. It's based in Munich, but has operations in over 70 countries and employs around 180,000 people.
3 Lee Byung-Chull began the business in 1938 as a trading company. It diversified into many areas, including food processing, textiles, retail, construction and shipbuilding. In 2012, the electronics arm of the company became the world's largest mobile-phone maker by unit sales. The headquarters are in Seoul, and it has over 400,000 employees worldwide.
4 As a boy in the 1920s in Sweden, Ingvar Kamprad started selling matches to his neighbours. He soon expanded into flower seeds, greeting cards, Christmas-tree decorations, pencils and pens. Later, he developed a furniture business, and in the 1960s came showrooms, self-assembly furniture and sales through catalogues. The group headquarters are in Liechtenstein.

Audio 36
started   lived   developed

Audio 37
based   expanded   hired   wanted
diversified   fired   manufactured   worked
employed   founded   produced

Audio 38
1 These are really coming into fashion now in this part of the world. As you see, they have high heels, they're made of leather and they come in four distinctive colours: white, purple, pink and black.
2 Your clients can use this app to connect your tablet to a whiteboard, so if you're doing a presentation, you can write or draw on the tablet and your audience will see it on the whiteboard. You can also save what you've done. It retails at 99 cents.
3 No need to take your car out to the car wash! With the Jetoff power washer, you can clean and polish your car at home. And not only that, it's multi-purpose. Use it for cleaning windows, walls, your path – even the roof. Only a metre long, with the tank holding eight litres of water, this handy gadget will keep …
4 Office moves can be a big headache for a business. But we can help you move office quickly and easily, while allowing you to continue your daily work. Our team of experts will work closely with you to identify first your needs and then the key steps required to make sure the operation is a success. Distance is never a problem. We have successfully completed hundreds of international relocations.

Audio 39
Interviewer: Moira, can you tell me about where you work?
Moira: I work at the headquarters of Realgame plc, in Newport, near Birmingham in England.
Interviewer: Is it a big company?
Moira: There are about 200 employees at our offices in Newport. But we're a subsidiary of Realtech, an American company, and the parent company is much bigger.
Interviewer: What does Realgame do?
Moira: We produce video games for the international market.
Interviewer: Can you tell me a little about the organisation of your company?
Moira: Yes, sure. At the top, there's the Board of Directors and under them, there's the Chief Executive Officer, John Gallo. Then there's Colette Jones – she's the Deputy CEO and Chief of Finance.

Audio scripts

Interviewer: And the company's divided into four business areas?
Moira: Yes. There are four departments, and each department has a director who reports to the CEO and Deputy. There's Tom Grant, who's responsible for technology with his IT Manager, Clare Finch. Then there's Steve Mason, the Operations Director. He has a Senior Producer reporting to him – Margaret Tyler. Next, there's the Business Development Director, Martin Newman. He works closely with Ally Simpson, the Public Relations Manager. And finally, there's Lisa Blake. She's in charge of the Art Department and she has an Assistant Art Director.
Interviewer: And who's that?
Moira: That's me!

Audio 40
1 assistant
2 manager
3 chief financial officer
4 cashier
5 software programmer
6 business development director
7 co-ordinator

Audio 41
1 You can contact me at my work e-mail address. It's mike dot carney – that's c-a-r-n-e-y at p-d-l power dot co dot uk.
2 If it's really urgent, you can get me through my personal e-mail: stuart – that's s-t-u-a-r-t – dash yip – y-i-p – at g-mail dot jn.
3 You can follow our company on Twitter at hashtag s-e-transport underscore shanghai, all lower case.
4 There's no problem with our website. We've just changed our domain name. It was w-w-w dot golf support dot com, but now it's w-w-w dot golf support dot e-u – golfsupport is all one word.
5 You can keep up to date with all your regional business news at w-w-w dot businessnews – all one word – dot com forward slash south america.
6 You can message us through Facebook – just search for asia foods forward slash Indonesia.
7 You can call me directly through Skype. My address is: rob-s 123 asterisk a-b-b.

Audio 42
/eɪ/	a, h, j, k
/iː/	b, c, d, e, g, p, t, v, z (AmE)
/e/	f, l, m, n, s, x, z (BrE)
/aɪ/	i, y
/əʊ/	o
/uː/	q, u, w
/ɑː/	r

Audio 43
Chairperson: So now let's move on to the next point on the agenda, Carters. As you know, Carters is one of our most important customers. But they're beginning to cause us problems, because they're so slow to pay. Let's go round the table for views on this. Tom?
Tom: We have to be very careful with them. We can't just call and tell them to pay now, they're too important to us. Unfortunately, I think we should wait. I know that's difficult, but …
  ***
Chairperson: Now, teamwork. Of course, teamwork's important to the company, but some people are saying that it's not right that they do all the work, while others who don't get the bonus too. Any ideas?
Su: Yes, we should look at each person's work. Why don't we have a system of individual bonuses, so you receive a bonus for the work you do?
Hans: No, I can't agree with that. The idea is to encourage teamwork, working in a team. Individual bonuses are a separate issue, we can't just …
  ***
Chairperson: Right, the trade fair in Hawaii in November. This seems to be very popular, but we can't all go – there are only three places. We should consider who really needs to be there.
Tom: Well, one of the people who's preparing our stand there should go, I think.
Su: I see what you mean, but really, as James said, we have to look at our aims. I mean, we want to sell, don't we? So the first person who has to go is …

Audio 44
1 I couldn't agree more.
2 What were you saying about delivery times?
3 Most people say they can't work in August.
4 We should concentrate on the issue of expense claims.
5 We aren't all in favour of that proposal.

Audio 45
a oh point two five
b a hundred
c a hundred and thirty
d four hundred and one
e one thousand, eight hundred and forty
f twenty-three thousand, six hundred and eighty-seven
g four hundred and eighty-nine thousand, five hundred and ninety-two
h four million, four hundred and twenty-seven thousand, three hundred and nine
i twelve million, two hundred and one thousand, three hundred and eighty-two
j eight billion

Audio 46
a sixty-eight euros and thirty-nine cents
b two hundred and ninety-eight dollars and thirty-eight cents
c five thousand four hundred and ninety-three pounds and ninety-three pence
d the third of June, twenty fifteen / the third of June, two thousand and fifteen
e March sixth, twenty fifteen / March sixth, two thousand fifteen
f forty-nine per cent
g a hundred per cent
h telephone oh-one-two-seven-three, five-double six-nine-three four
i sixty-six kilometres per hour
j a quarter
k a third
l a half
m three-quarters
n a tenth

Audio 47
sixteen	sixty	seventeen	seventy
thirteen	thirty	eighteen	eighty
fourteen	forty	nineteen	ninety
fifteen	fifty		

Audio 48
1 The average share price in March was 386 Japanese yen.
2 In April, unemployment went down by 486,000.
3 Sales went up in the last quarter to 146,500.
4 They put up the price by $5.
5 There was a drop of 13% in the number of new orders.
6 269 divided by 2 equals 134.5.
7 Two-thirds of customers in the taste test thought our product was the best.
8 **Man:** You're driving too fast.
  Woman: No, I'm not! I'm going at 130 kilometres per hour.
  Man: Yes, but the speed limit's 120 kilometres per hour!

Audio 49
… as you can see from the bar graph, the launch of our BZ1 wasn't a huge success at the start of the year. We sold only 30,000 models in January, and sales remained steady at this level in February. However, we all know that motorbike sales are seasonal and, with the improved weather in March, they increased by more than a hundred per cent to 80,000. There was more good news in April, when they went up again by 20,000. But then something went wrong. May was very disappointing, as there was a fall of 50 per cent to 50,000, and again in June, when sales fell from 50,000 to 20,000, the lowest figure of the year. Why did this happen, and what can we do about it?

Audio scripts

Audio 50
Sales went up by 10%.
Production went down on average.
There was a fall in the figures.
Sales increased in January.
Percentages remained stable at 6%.

Audio 51
Host: Hello! Come in. Lovely to see you again. Let me take your coat.
Guest: Shall I leave my shoes here?
Host: Yes, please.
Guest: I've brought you this little present.
Host: Oh, that's very kind of you. Tulips! Beautiful … Come through to the living room. Make yourself at home.
Guest: Thank you.
Host: Can I get you something to drink? Some tea, coffee or a cold drink?
Guest: Yes, could I have a cup of tea, please?
Host: Sure, how do you like it?
Guest: Er, one sugar, please – no milk.
Host: Did you have any trouble finding the way here?
Guest: No, it was easy. I used the sat-nav.
Guest: Could you tell me where the toilet is, please?
Host: Yes, of course, it's this way.
***
Guest: Well, thank you very much for the tea and the cake. It was delicious. But it's getting late. I really should go.
Host: It was nice to see you.
Guest: You must come to my house the next time you're in Sydney.
Host: I'd love to, thanks.

Audio 52
1 see you again – Nice to see you again.
2 kind of you – That's very kind of you.
3 at home – Make yourself at home.
4 your coffee? – like your coffee? – How do you like your coffee?
5 for the tea – Thank you very much for the tea.
6 late – It's getting late.

Audio 53
Interviewer: So, Mansour, can you tell us about McDonald's and their marketing mix?
Mansour: Well, if we look at Product first, the procedure for deciding on the menu begins with market research. They want to know which items the customer wants to see on the menu. In fact, they do market research continuously. Some products might be popular today, but not tomorrow. They are at different points in their lifecycles, and McDonald's keeps an eye on this.
Interviewer: And how do they promote their products?
Mansour: They use lots of ways – for example, they advertise on TV, online, in the cinema, using in-store promotions and loyalty schemes. The trick is to combine these in a way that produces the best results. So the customer can get to learn about the product on TV, see more details of it in the press; then there will be an in-store promotion to get people to try it with maybe a gift to collect … So people will buy it again and so on. They play as a team.
Interviewer: They have low pricing, don't they?
Mansour: Of course. McDonald's uses competitive pricing, but when they decide on a price, they know it's important not to go too low – so low that profits are reduced too much or the idea of quality in the mind of the customer is questioned.
Interviewer: What about Place?
Mansour: Place is the most important 'P' for McDonald's. Remember, they reach around 52 million customers a day. Nearly 50% of the US is less than three minutes away from their nearest McDonald's, so of course the company tries to create an environment that the customer enjoys.
Interviewer: Like the kids' playground areas.
Mansour: Yes, you can find these in their restaurants all over the world.

Audio 54
Seller: This is our new range of phone accessories, including cases, headphones and earbuds. The cases come in four colours. They're very popular at the moment. We've sold out of them twice this year, so if you're interested, it might be a good idea to order early.
Customer: Yes, maybe the cases and earphones, but not the earbuds. We've already got too many in stock. Have you got your price list?
Seller: Yes, here you are.
Customer: What kind of discount can you give me on the cases?
Seller: The unit price is four euros twenty-five, but you've been a good customer this year, so I'd like to offer you a discount of 18 per cent on orders over 300.
Customer: How about 20 per cent?
Seller: All right. Would you like to order today?
Customer: Let's start with the cases and we'll see how they go.
Seller: How many?
Customer: Three hundred. When can you deliver?
Seller: We can get them to you by next Friday.
Customer: OK.
Seller: Now, those earbuds … have you thought about changing brand? I can tell you that the ones you have there sell much less well than these. I can show you the national figures here—
Customer: Yes, I'm sure you can, Jack, but I just haven't got the time at the moment!

Audio 55
1	price	prize	5	weight	wait	9	whole	hole
2	sell	sale	6	by	buy	10	work	walk
3	right	write	7	knows	nose			
4	it	eat	8	tell	tail			

Audio 56
1 These bags fit straight into the trolley. At the checkout, the shoppers can put the items they've bought straight into the bags and then unload the bags directly into the car. It saves waste on carrier bags, too.
2 We have some very good customers who really like our service. They're young social-media followers, and we know they're always happy to make comments, re-tweet messages and click likes. They give a lot of momentum to our brand.
3 We provide a complete service of car fleets to corporate clients. We take care of the purchase of the cars, the financing, insurance, maintenance, licensing, fuel … everything.

Audio 57
1 Can you tell me about your customers?
2 They're mainly women and they work at home.
3 They're from cities.
4 Where do they live?
5 This group is aged from 20 to 40.
6 Does she work for a bank?

Audio 58
Anja: We import, pack and sell high-quality chocolates. I would say that the internet allows us to find new customers, and our existing customers can access our website for product information. I mean, they can get detailed information, so that they can make a complete order over the net. Those with a password can log on and follow the progress of their orders. I think this has meant a considerable improvement in our quality of service.
Gabriela: Our company operates internationally, but I'd say that our key business depends more than ever on personal contact. Phone and face-to-face contacts are still very important for us. However, yes, the internet's important for lots of reasons: finding new customers is one, and visitors who browse our site can access a lot of useful information, so it creates good PR. The internet's also essential for internal communications, of course. Management consultants spend a long time away from the office, so we always use e-mail and Skype to keep in touch with each other.

Audio scripts

Joe: We're in a downtown location here, and most of our business is take-out or delivery. Since most of our lunchtime customers are busy businesspeople with the internet in front of them, we've set up our own Pizza Pan website. Customers order over the net, and we deliver it to their workstations.
Interviewer: How does that work exactly?
Joe: It's easy – you just go to our homepage, scroll down to menus, choose your pizza, click on the link to order and that's it. It's very user-friendly, and I think it's good advertising, too. I've checked out a few other take-out restaurants near here with websites, but they aren't nearly as good as ours.

Audio 59

Woman 1: Look, Margot has been our most successful sales executive for the last two years. I don't think we should stop her – the opposite, in fact. I think we should give her a bonus or a prize!
Man: Could I just say something here? I know Margot's a good sales executive, but the others are saying that they could sell the same if they gave customers the kinds of gift that Margot does.
Woman 2: Well, why don't they?
Man: Because it's against the company rules!
Woman 1: Margot's sold more this year than any of the—
Man: If I could just finish … There's a company rule which says you can't give customers presents worth more than $150. That's the maximum.
Woman 2: Ah. So you're saying Margot is the best sales executive because she's the only one who breaks the company rules on gifts?
Man: Exactly.
Woman 2: Well, in that case, it seems we'll have to stop her.
Woman 1: Just a minute, what's the value of the gifts that Margot has made compared with the profit from her sales? If the profit's much bigger, then maybe we should think about changing the company rules on gifts instead.
Woman 2: Yes, that's a possibility, isn't it? Can you look into that, Cora?
Woman 1: Yes, sure.
Woman 2: So let's wait until we have more information before we make a decision on this.

Audio 60
/æ/ ran   /ʌ/ run

Audio 61
1 cat   cut   4 began   begun
2 fan   fun   5 drank   drunk
3 match much

Audio 62
/e/ end   /æ/ and

Audio 63
1 men   man   4 any   Annie
2 head   had   5 bed   bad
3 said   sad

Audio 64
First of all, the image of the object you want to make is designed on the computer using special software. When it's finished, the information is sent from the computer to the 3D printer. You can make objects in over a hundred different materials, so the next thing is to decide which material you want to make the object with and program the printer. Then you start the printing, and the object is created in layers, like slices of bread. Finally, the material is usually hardened by a laser, and that's it.

Audio 65
1 pro<u>duce</u>   <u>pro</u>duct   pro<u>du</u>cer   pro<u>duc</u>tion   pro<u>duc</u>tive
2 com<u>pete</u>   compe<u>ti</u>tion   com<u>pe</u>titor   com<u>pe</u>titive
3 <u>ad</u>vertise   <u>ad</u>vertising   ad<u>ver</u>tisement

Audio 66
The customer called us last Friday and made an enquiry about our XT printers. We spoke, and they asked for a quote on 18 machines. We gave them a quote of €1,800. They asked about the delivery date, but I wasn't sure about our stock level, so I said I would call them back. I checked the stock, and we had the printers. I called them and told them they could have the machines in four days. They accepted and sent us an order by e-mail. I then invoiced them for the full amount, and we dispatched the shipment by lorry from our warehouse that afternoon. It reached the customer after three days.

Audio 67
container   courier   director   distributor   inspector   order   retailer   sender   receiver   wholesaler

Audio 68
1 Sorry I'm late.
2 Excuse me, do you know where Bond Street is?
3 No, let me, please!
4 Would you like to come to dinner this evening?
5 Excuse me.
6 Can you tell me what time breakfast is, please?
7 How long does it take to get to the airport?
8 A single to Paris, please.
9 Oh, I'm sorry. I'll get you another one.
10 Bye! Have a good weekend!
11 My car's got a flat tyre, and I haven't got a spare.
12 Could I have a receipt, please?
13 Can I charge my phone here?
14 Sorry? Could you say that again?
15 Would you like a lift to the airport?
16 They're too big. Can I try on a smaller size?

Audio 69
17 No, not at all.
18 Yes, sure. Go ahead.
19 You're welcome.
20 Thanks, I'll need it!
21 Yes, please – at seven o'clock.
22 Let's go to the cinema.
23 Fine. And you?
24 Nice to meet you.
25 Black with one sugar, please.
26 Thanks, you too!
27 Congratulations!
28 Oh no! You must be joking!
29 Nice to meet you too.
30 It's raining.
31 Go to the end of the corridor. It's the last door on the right.
32 Yes, sure.
33 Yes, it's on the second floor.
34 Yes, it's half past two.
35 Shall I get you an aspirin?
36 Very short at the sides but quite long on the top. Like Rihanna!

Audio 70
Twenty-four-year-old Katie Lao had the idea while she was watering her only plant during her final year at Toronto University in 2007. She created a plant food made entirely from organic food waste. She noticed there was nothing like this on the market and decided that she should try to develop her idea. Her parents helped her to set up a company, Cyclaterra, package her product and try to promote it, but she had soon spent all the money she had. She didn't give up, although sales were very slow and she was starting to get worried. Then one day, she was invited to take part in a radio interview. A caller to the programme was very interested and soon after invested 5,000 dollars in Katie's new business. A month later, sales took off. Today, some of Cyclaterra's 15 products are found in several of the largest supermarket chains.

Audio 71
/s/   products   parents   several   contracts   sorry
/z/   dollars   Katie's   deserved   years   was

Audio scripts

Audio 72
/s/ slow some soon supermarket this
/z/ chains congratulations result these

Audio 73/74
Shall we start? Good morning, everybody. The reason we're here today is to decide on a number of important issues. Does everybody have a copy of the agenda? Good. Let's start with all the rumours around the office about job cuts. I know a lot of us are very worried about this, but is there any truth in these stories? …

Let's look at the next point now: Susan Wren and the problem of George Blake again. If we aren't careful, this is going to become a legal problem. So what do you suggest we do about Blake? Any ideas?

So … let's move on to the complaints we've had from the finance department about expense claims. What can be claimed as expenses and what can't? I think that's an important question to sort out …

And finally, the car park. This has been a problem for some years now. Let's go round the table on this – Jessica, what do you think?

Audio 75
Woman: The City Star's lighter than the Lux because it's made of carbon fibre, but it's not the lightest.
Man: No, the Cavendish is the lightest – it's ten kilos.
Woman: Yeah, the weight's quite important, because I'll need to carry it up and downstairs at the office.
Man: Comfort: the Lux is the most comfortable.
Woman: Yes, and the City Star's more comfortable than the Cavendish. That's good, considering the price.
Man: Wheel size: the Cavendish has got nice big wheels.
Woman: The Lux's are only 40 centimetres, the same as the City Star's.
Man: Well, that's not too bad, is it?
Woman: Folding time – that's important. I have to get on and off the train with it, so the Lux takes ten seconds, whereas the Cavendish only takes four seconds – wow!
Man: Yes, but look at the price. It's the best bike, but it's the most expensive, of course.
Woman: Mmm, I like this one – the City Star. But $850, that's a lot …
Man: Well, you aren't paying. I am.
Woman: What do you mean?
Man: It's your birthday next week, isn't it?
Woman: Yes, but …
Man: But what?
Woman: Nothing. Thank you, you're the best husband in the world!

Audio 76
1 The City Star's lighter than the Lux.
2 It's better than the bigger one.
3 This film's older than that one.
4 The size is the same as the blue bike.

Audio 77
1 doubled
2 compared
3 reached
4 changed
5 increased
6 decreased

Audio 78
The total global market for car sharing should continue to grow strongly. Since the early days, customers have preferred ride-sharing compared to street rental services, and the private-driver service is expected to keep its greater share of the market.
However, according to the forecast, both street rental and ride-sharing might start to fall slightly in 2027 due to the introduction of robotic car services. While ride-sharing will continue to be the market leader till 2028, at this point robotic car services might overtake them. By 2030, it is expected that most passengers will choose a robot to drive them.

Audio 79
Woman: Things like smartphones have made it easier for companies to communicate with employees, and staff can always check in with the office. Besides voice calls, they can use e-mailing and instant messaging, as well as connecting to social-networking services to encourage communication across departments. The problem is that people send too many unnecessary internal e-mails – my inbox is always full! More importantly, it means that employees are always connected to their work – 24/7. This creates tiring conditions, which in turn can lead to low morale and poor productivity.
Man: I guess that all this new technology can really improve productivity. Think about your tablet – it's got so many apps – maps, calendars, contact lists – all instantly available to use! And you can check information with your office wherever you are in the world. The downside of this is all the distractions. You've got games, video sites, social networking and personal e-mail. I think you could spend all day using all of these things and produce absolutely nothing of value!
Woman: To me, improved customer service is the most important thing about communication technology. You don't need to waste time and money going to visit customers to fix problems or to get information – with my laptop, I can access their servers remotely and do all this from my office. But I do think there's a problem with this. Security – is our data really safe?

Audio 80
1 Staff can always check their e-mails.
2 This can lead to low morale.
3 New technology can really improve productivity.
4 I can access their servers remotely.

Audio 81
1 Japan   Japanese
2 Italy   Italian
3 China   Chinese
4 Vietnam   Vietnamese
5 Europe   European
6 Egypt   Egyptian

Audio 82
The economy of New Zealand is mostly agricultural. Its main exports include meat, dairy products, forestry products, fruit, vegetables, fish and wool. Currently, the main manufacturing industries are machinery, textiles and food processing. Energy is not expensive, and 82 per cent of electricity is produced from renewables.
The service sector is also vital to the economy. New Zealand is a beautiful country, and more than two million tourists visit the country every year.
On the whole, the economy is in quite a good condition compared to a lot of other countries. It's growing at about one per cent a year. In 2016, GDP grew by 0.8 per cent, with unemployment at four and a half per cent.
Finally, one great thing about living in New Zealand is taxation. It has the second lowest tax rate in the world, after Chile!

Audio 83
1 economy   economics   economical
2 industry   industrial
3 agriculture   agricultural
4 manufacture   manufacturing

Answer key

Unit 1

1 1 e 2 a 3 b 4 f 5 c 6 d

2 1 B 2 A 3 F 4 C 5 D 6 E

5 1 Quality Inspector 2 Newcastle 3 Full-time 4 raw materials
5 finished products 6 Inspect the quality of the packaging

7
1 Who do you work for?
2 What's your job title?
3 What's the main purpose of your job?
4 What other responsibilities do you have?
5 Where are you based?
6 Which department do you work in?
7 Do you work full-time or part-time?
8 Are you in / Have you got / Is it / Do you have a temporary or (a) permanent position?
9 Who do you report to?
10 Do you like your job? Why?
11 What did you do before this job?
12 What would you like to do in the future?

Unit 2

1 *Suggested answers*
1 mobile phone / text / WhatsApp message
2 e-mail
3 social media / Skype
4 e-mail / social media
5 e-mail / social media
6 face to face

3 **internal contacts:** managers, colleagues, other department personnel
external contacts: customers/clients, suppliers

4
1 T
2 F (She talks to them about design.)
3 T
4 F (She talks to them / discusses things with them.)
5 F (The Public Relations department does this.)

Pronunciation 1 /tuː/: 3, 5, 7; /tə/: 1, 2, 4, 6, 8

5 1 told/asked 2 said 3 say/ask 4 told/asked 5 tell
6 told/asked

6 1 discusses 2 agree 3 calls 4 argues 5 face to face
6 talked

Unit 3

1 See audio script 5 on page 89.

3
1 The order reference should be 180-G-7; the phone number should be 098-63-263.
2 The buses are on strike, not the trains.

Unit 4

1

	10.00	11.00	13.00	15.00	16.00
Mr Blue	✔				
Ms Scarlet				✔	
Mr Brown and Ms Pink			✔		
Mr Black					✔
Ms Orange				✔	

3 Answers in bold are those used in the recording.
1 **How**/What about
2 **Are you free** / What are you doing
3 **'m busy all day** / can't make it
4 **Would three o'clock suit you?** / Are you free at three o'clock? / Shall we say three o'clock?
5 So/**OK**

5

at	on	in
five o'clock	20th March	2015
half past three	Wednesday	April
the weekend (BrE)	Tuesday afternoon	the afternoon
	the weekend (AmE)	June

Unit 5

1 *Suggested answers*
1 Please take/have a seat.
2 Did you have a good trip/journey?
3 Would you like to come to lunch with us?
4 Would you like a/some coffee?
5 'This is Carl.' 'How do you do?'
6 I look forward to seeing you again next month.

2
1 F (They haven't met before, so they introduce themselves.)
2 T
3 T
4 F (He had no problems on the trip.)
5 T
6 F (They'll meet in July.)

3 All the Key language expressions are used except:
How was your flight?
Is this your first visit to Birmingham/Madrid?

Pronunciation
1 A: Pleased **to** meet you!
   B: Pleased **to** meet you too!
2 A: Would you like **a** coffee or tea?
   B: **A** coffee, please!
3 A: Did you have **a** good trip?
   B: Not really. What about you?
4 A: How **was** your flight?
   B: Not too bad, thanks.
5 A: It **was** nice meeting you!
   B: Thanks, you too!

4 *Suggested answers*
1 How do you do?
2 Nice to meet you too.
3 A tea, please.
4 Nice to meet you, Mr Lau.
5 Yes, it was fine, thanks.
6 No, not yet.
7 Yes, it's very nice, thank you.
8 You too.

Unit 6

1 1 hard skills 2 soft skills

2 Soft skills: 1, 3, 5
Hard skills: 2, 4, 6

Pronunciation 2

/z/	/s/	/ð/	/θ/
organi**s**ed	**s**ome	**th**en	**th**ing
language**s**	progre**ss**ing	o**th**er	**th**in
plea**s**e	**s**ay	**th**eir	
pre**s**entation	**s**oft	wi**th**	
	sale		
	speak		
	fa**c**e		

5 1 pressure 2 take criticism 3 positive attitude 4 organised
5 initiative 6 flexible

97

Answer key

Unit 7

2 1 aim today   2 feel free to interrupt   3 I've divided   4 we'll look   5 Let's begin/start

Pronunciation 1
1 won't   2 I'd   3 Don't   4 let's   5 you're   6 've   7 'll   8 I'm

Unit 8

1 *Suggested answers*
Good advice: 1, 2
Bad advice: 3 (Focus on someone at the front of the room.); 5 (It can be distracting if you move around too much.); 7 (Practising beforehand will help you feel more confident.)
It depends: 4 (Sometimes it can be better for people to ask questions as you go along.); 6 (Jokes can help break the ice, but not everyone shares the same sense of humour, so you have to be careful.)

3   1   F (It produces drinking water from salt water.)
   2   T
   3   T
   4   F (He wants to invest in marketing and promotion.)
   5   T

4   Let's move on to …
   Now we come to …
   The reason for this is …
   compared to
   To sum up, …
   Finally, …

Pronunciation 2
See audio script 17 on page 90.

Unit 9

2   travelling: 3 hours (not 2 hours)
   computer and phone: 3 hours (not 4 hours)

4   1 by   2 spent   3 late   4 wasted   5 save   6 took
   7 delayed/postponed   8 meet

Pronunciation 1
1 debt   2 gate   3 we'll   4 its   5 bin   6 west   7 sleep   8 this

Pronunciation 2

/e/ as in *spend*	/eɪ/ as in *late*	/ɪ/ as in *list*	/iː/ as in *be*
debt	date	will	we'll
get	gate	its	eats
west	waste	bin	been
slept		this	sleep
			these

Unit 10

1   c, e, d, a, b

2   *Suggested answers*
   They began contacting customers / advertising.
   They recruited staff to help them.

3   Three

4   1   T
   2   F (They ask about work experience.)
   3   T
   4   F (They meet people from HR and Finance.)
   5   T

5   1 ~~steps~~ stages   2 ~~in-depth~~ detailed   3 ~~discover~~ find out
   4 ~~pay~~ salary   5 ~~for four~~ a few

Pronunciation 1
The speaker pauses after the following words:
1 all   2 So   3 Then; interview   4 that   5 finally

6   *Suggested answer*
   First of all, find out as much as you can about the company offering the job.
   Then prepare questions to ask during the interview.
   Next, answer the questions clearly and honestly.
   After that, practise the interview with a friend.
   Then dress for the interview as you would for the job.
   Next, find out exactly where you have to go.
   Finally, make sure you aren't late.

Unit 11

1   *Suggested answer*
   He's stressed because of work pressures (e.g. falling sales). His attempt to get away from it all results in the same situation happening again.

4   Work, money, relationships

5   1 as a result   2 due to stress, so
   3 under too much pressure   4 need to   5 prioritise

Pronunciation
Silent letters: *talk* (l), *psychologist* (p, h), *straight* (gh), *would* (l), *resign* (g), *listen* (t), *Wednesday* (d, e), *doubt* (b), *mortgage* (t)

6   I feel much better because of my new schedule.
   She woke up late because she went to bed late, so she was late for work again.
   He's stressed as a result of the pressure he's under at work.
   She feels under pressure as a result of problems with her colleagues, so she's decided to resign.
   I get stressed due to my work deadlines. Consequently, I often have headaches.

Unit 12

2   Order c

3   Sea bass is a kind of fish.
   It's cooked in …
   Does it come with …?
   What do you recommend?
   I'd like the …
   I'll have the …
   Could I have …?
   I'll have the same.
   Would you like …?

4   1 a   2 c   3 d   4 b   5 e

5   1 prawns   2 onions   3 mushrooms   4 red pepper
   5 aubergine   6 olives   7 cabbage   8 carrots   9 peas
   10 garlic   11 raspberries   12 grapes

Pronunciation 1

/eɪ/ as in *day*	/aɪ/ as in *fine*	/əʊ/ as in *no*	/aʊ/ as in *out*	/ɪə/ as in *here*
baked	buy	grow	now	beer
cake	fried	know	our	hear
change	I'll	show	shower	near
grape	rice	smoked	sound	
main	right			
same	wine			
straight				
waiter				

Unit 13

1 *Suggested answer*

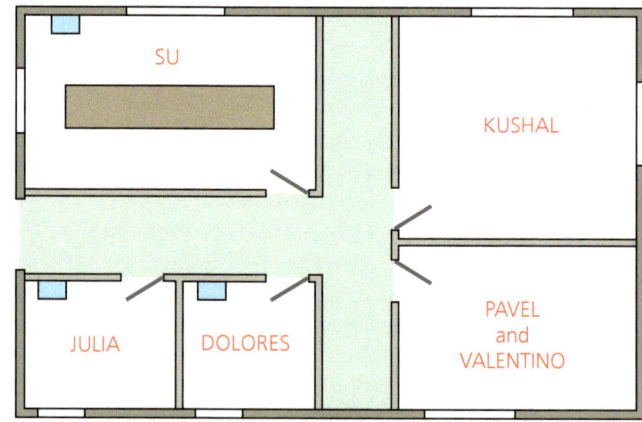

3   Summary b

98

Answer key

4 *Suggested answers*
As we often don't have the goods in stock, there are delivery delays to customers.
Our computer system is very slow because it's ten years old.
I was late for the meeting because I missed the train.
The reason why I haven't had a salary increase for three years is that business hasn't been good.
We're spending too much on supplies from the USA because of the high price of the dollar.
As there is a very high staff turnover, people often don't follow projects through from beginning to end.

Pronunciation 1
Suggested answers
Their <u>father</u> didn't want to set up a <u>website</u> because of the <u>cost</u>.
As the <u>cost</u> was <u>high</u>, their <u>father</u> didn't want to set up a <u>website</u>.

Unit 14

2 *Suggested answers*
1 Do you know when the train leaves?
2 Can you tell me where the station is?
3 Can you tell me which train I have to get?
4 Do you know what time it is?
5 Could you tell me how this ticket machine works?
6 Could you tell which terminal the flight leaves from?

3 *Suggested answers*
1 The train is arriving in Paris / at the Gare du Nord.
2 He's going by car.
3 She's getting into a taxi.
4 He's booking/buying a ticket.
5 They're getting on a plane.
6 They're going by train. They're getting on/off a train.

4 See audio script 31 on page 92.

Unit 15

Pronunciation 2
1 I'm going **to** look **for a** new job.
2 She comes **from** Berlin.
3 I went **to** school in France.
4 Are you going **to** stay in this job **for** long?

2 1 f 2 i 3 d 4 g 5 e 6 c 7 a 8 h 9 b 10 j

Unit 16

1
- Allianz: financial services; head office in Munich, Germany; founded in Germany by Carl von Thieme and Wilhelm von Finck in 1890
- BP: gas and petroleum; head office in London, England; originally APOC (founded in 1909), became BP in 1954
- Gazprom: gas; head office in Moscow, Russia; founded in the former Soviet Union by the Soviet government in 1989
- eBay: online marketplace; head office in San José, USA; founded in the USA by Pierre Omidyar in 1995
- IKEA: self-assembly furniture and home furnishings; head office in Liechtenstein, the Netherlands; founded in Sweden by Ingvar Kamprad in 1943
- Samsung: trading company with many arms; head office in Seoul, South Korea; founded in South Korea by Lee Byung-Chull in 1938
- Unilever: food and personal consumer goods; head offices in London, UK, and Rotterdam, the Netherlands; founded in the Netherlands in 1929
- Toyota: vehicle manufacturer; head office in Aichi, Japan; founded in Japan by Kiichiro Toyoda in 1937

2 1 eBay 2 Allianz 3 Samsung 4 IKEA

3 1 Allianz 2 eBay 3 Samsung 4 IKEA 5 Samsung

Pronunciation 2

/ɪd/	/d/	/t/
expanded	diversified	based
founded	employed	produced
wanted	fired	worked
	hired	
	manufactured	

4
1 What does the company produce?
2 What services does the company provide?
3 Where is it based?
4 How many sites has the company got?
5 When did it begin?
6 Who started it?
7 How did it start?
8 How did it develop?
9 How many employees are there?
10 How is it performing at the moment?

Unit 17

3 a removals   b spraying/cleaning   c window cleaning
d whiteboard   e boots/footwear   f tablet/computing

4 1 e 2 f 3 b 4 a

5 *Suggested answers*
1 It's for mixing food.
2 It's for making coffee.
3 It's for cooking/frying food.
4 It's for making toast / toasting bread.
5 It's for weighing food/ingredients.
6 It's for opening bottles / taking corks out.

Unit 18

1 1 *Suggested answer*
Because there are no clear reporting lines – there will be many relationships across the company, often crisscrossing each other with no hierarchy, like a plate of spaghetti.

2 1 plc   2 CEO   3 Chief of Finance
4 Operations   5 Public Relations   6 Assistant

3
1 In the USA
2 Yes, it produces video games for the international market.
3 The whole company
4 The CEO and Deputy CEO

Unit 19

2 1 c 2 a 3 g 4 b 5 f 6 i 7 h 8 e 9 d

3
1 mike.carney@pdlpower.co.uk
2 stuart-yip@gmail.jn
3 #setransport_shanghai
4 (*old*) www.golfsupport.com; (*new*) www.golfsupport.eu
5 www.businessnews.com/southamerica
6 asiafoods/indonesia
7 robs123*abb

Pronunciation 1 See audio script 42 on page 93.

Pronunciation 2 *a, e, i, o, u* (and in some words *y*)

Unit 20

3 1 c 2 a 3 b

4
1 Let's go round the table for views on this.
2 I think we should
3 Any ideas?
4 Why don't we
5 I can't agree with that
6 I see what you mean

Pronunciation 1
1 couldn't   2 were   3 can't   4 should   5 aren't

Unit 21

1 *Sample answers*
1 The twenty-eighth of July / July twenty-eighth, nineteen ninety-four

Answer key

2. The seventh of February / February seventh, twenty nineteen / two thousand and nineteen
3. Three hundred (and) sixty-five
4. Ninety-five thousand pounds
5. Four hundred thousand
6. Sixty-six million
7. Oh-one-double eight-three, two-nine-six, four-three-five
8. Sixty-four per cent

2
- a oh/zero/nought point two five
- b a/one hundred
- c a/one hundred and thirty
- d four hundred (and) one
- e one thousand, eight hundred (and) forty
- f twenty-three thousand, six hundred (and) eighty-seven
- g four hundred and eighty-nine thousand, five hundred (and) ninety-two
- h four million, four hundred and twenty-seven thousand, three hundred (and) nine
- i twelve million, two hundred and one thousand, three hundred (and) eighty-two
- j eight billion

3
- a sixty-eight euros (and) thirty-nine cents
- b two hundred and ninety-eight dollars (and) thirty-eight cents
- c five thousand four hundred and ninety-three pounds (and) ninety-three pence
- d the third of June, twenty fifteen / two thousand and fifteen
- e March sixth, twenty fifteen / two thousand fifteen
- f forty-nine per cent
- g a/one hundred per cent
- h telephone oh-one-two-seven-three, five-double six-nine-three-four
- i sixty-six kilometres per/an hour
- j a/one quarter
- k a/one third
- l a/one half
- m three-quarters
- n a/one tenth

Pronunciation 1
The stress is on the second syllable in column A and the first syllable in column B.

4   1 ✔   2 486,000   3 146,500   4 ✔   5 13%   6 134.5
    7 ²⁄₃   8 ✔

5

Student A's invoice	Student B's invoice
Tel. 01273 55982	Tel. 01273 55983
Account no. BRN887	Account no. BRN877
Invoice date: 22/10/19	Invoice date: 22/11/19
Product code: KJ15	Product code: KJ50
Discount: £1,965.02	Discount: £1,865.02
Total due: £17,685.18	Total due: £17,785.18

6 In Student B's invoice, the 10% discount has been miscalculated.

Unit 22

1 The blue line (As the number of hours increases, productivity decreases due to tiredness, etc.)

2

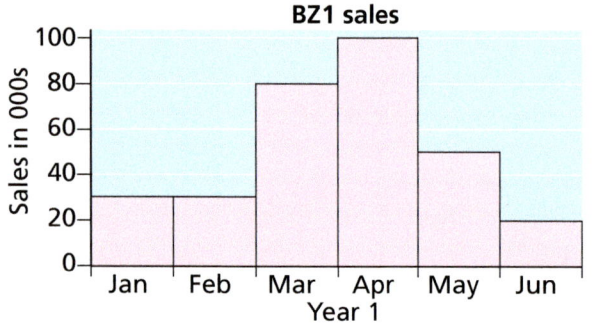

3

↘	→	↗
dropped	remained stable	has risen
fell	stayed constant	increased
has fallen		rose
went down		went up

Unit 23

1 All are generally true.

2 Hello! Come in. Lovely/Nice to see you again. H
Let me take your coat. H
Shall I leave my shoes here? G
I've brought you this little present. G
That's very kind of you. H
Come through to the living room. H
Make yourself at home / comfortable. H
Can I get you something to drink? / Would you like a …? H
Yes, could I have … , please. G
How do you like your tea/coffee? H
One sugar, please – no milk. G
Did you have any trouble finding the way here? H
No, it was easy. I used the sat-nav. G
Could you tell me where the toilet/bathroom is, please? G
Thank you very much for the tea/lunch, etc. G
It's getting late. I really should go. G
It was nice to see you. H/G
You must come to my house the next time you're in … G

4 *Suggested answers*
1 in   2 you again   3 your coat   4 my shoes here
5 you this little present   6 kind of you   7 through to   8 at home
9 you something to drink   10 coffee or a soft drink
11 'd love some/a   12 do you like
13 Milk and one sugar, please   14 finding the way   15 easy
16 the toilet is   17 that door over there   18 getting
19 should go

Unit 24

1 1 Price   2 Promotion   3 Place   4 Product

3 Place

4 1 see   2 today; tomorrow   3 on; in-store
4 on; low   5 52; 50%; three

5 1 d   2 i   3 f   4 b   5 g   6 e   7 h   8 c   9 a

Unit 25

1 because, free, instant, new, you

3 1 Product c   2 300

4 I'd like to offer you …
Have you thought about …?
It might be a good idea to …
They're very popular.

Pronunciation 1   3, 5, 6, 7, 9

5 1 to offer a discount   2 list price   3 price list   4 to invoice
5 to close a deal   6 unit price   7 to sell out   8 sales rep
9 range of goods

Unit 26

1 *Suggested answers*
Harrods opened in London in 1824 and is the largest department store in Europe. It is currently owned by the state of Qatar. Customers are typically socio-economic class A. It also attracts a lot of tourists.
Primark is an Irish fast-fashion retailer with its headquarters in Dublin. Its customers are price sensitive, often families.
Hollister is an American chain aimed at the teenage market. The stores have dark interiors and play loud music. Its products are a little cheaper than its parent company, Abercrombie and Fitch.
Gucci was founded by Guccio Gucci in Florence, Italy, in 1921. It has 278 stores worldwide and sells mainly fashion and leather goods. Customers are socio-economic class A and B, mainly women aged 20 to 50.

Answer key

3 *Suggested answers*
a She's a young woman, probably about 20 years old. She looks smart, so she's probably a professional. I think she's single, from somewhere in Europe.
b He's a corporate customer. He's middle-aged and comes from Asia. He probably earns a high salary.
c She's probably middle income. She's buying a lot of shopping. She's probably married as she has at least one child. She might work in an office or she could be a housewife.
d They're married and elderly. They're retired, they're probably middle income.

4 1 c   2 a   3 b

5 1 a   2 b

6 1 b   2 a   3 a   4 b   5 a

Unit 27

1 1 c   2 d   3 a   4 f   5 b   6 g   7 e

3 1 search for   2 log onto   3 user-friendly
4 set up / designed   5 order over   6 access

5

	Anja Winter	Gabriela Silva	Joe Turati
buying or selling	✔		✔
database			
public relations, providing information	✔	✔	
training staff			
marketing, finding new customers	✔	✔	✔
customer service	✔		
doing research			
communicating with employees		✔	
watching competitors			✔
advertising jobs			

6 1 T
2 F (The opposite is true for her business.)
3 T
4 T

Unit 28

1 1 held   2 attended   3 absent; apologies   4 Point
5 adjourned   6 postpone   7 bring forward

3 1 F (For two years)
2 T
3 T
4 F (They decide to wait till they have more information.)

4 Could I just say something here?
If I could just finish …
Yes, that's a possibility.
Let's wait until we have more information.
So you're saying …

5 *Suggested answers*
1 If I could just finish what I was saying, …
2 Going back to the point about the marketing budget, …
3 Could I just say something here?
4 So what you're suggesting is that we wait for the next quarter's figures before making a decision.
5 Sorry, could you repeat that last point again?
6 Let's wait until we have more information.

Unit 29

1 workers, assembly line, conveyor belt, semi-finished products, industrial robots, finished goods, packed, pallet, fork-lift truck, machinery

2 *Suggested answer*
It's a factory. They're manufacturing computers on an assembly line. Robots are assembling the computers, which are moving on a conveyor belt. A man driving a fork-lift truck is arriving with some boxes on a pallet. Another man seems to be supervising.

3 c, e, a, d, b

Pronunciation
See audio script 65 on page 95 for stressed syllables.
The different stresses are:
1 product   2 competition   3 advertisement

5 There are six.

6 1 The goods are sent by lorry.
2 The order is sent by e-mail.
3 The cars are made in Warsaw.
4 The quality of the raw materials is checked in the factory.
5 The fruit is sold in supermarkets.
6 The goods are packed in cardboard boxes.

7 *Suggested answers*
Student A
Two or three colours are made invidually.
Two separate compartments at the top of the tube are filled with colours.
The rest of the tube is filled with white toothpaste.
The white and colours are mixed when the tube is squeezed.
Student B
A bottle is put over a baby pear and the bottle is tied to the branch.
It is taken down when the pear has grown.
The bottle and pear are washed by hand.
The bottle is filled with brandy.

Unit 30

1 *Suggested answers*
1 I'd ship them by container.
2 I'd send it by courier.
3 I'd contact the nearest refrigerated warehouse and arrange to store the cheese there.
4 I'd transport him by road and ship.

3 1 enquiry   2 quote €1,800   3 check stock   4 4 days
5 order   6 invoice   7 lorry   8 customer

4 to make an enquiry
to ask for a quote
to send an order (for some goods)
to invoice (a customer)
to check the stock
to dispatch a shipment

5 1 They delivered the shipment by lorry (BrE) / truck (AmE).
2 The cargo arrived in Hong Kong by container ship.
3 We're in a hurry, so I've sent the parcel by courier.
4 to track your order (online)
5 The van was loaded at the warehouse and unloaded at the offices.
6 We send valuable goods by air freight.

Pronunciation 1
The schwa sound is in the final syllable of each word (the suffix –er/–or).

Unit 31

See audio scripts 68 and 69 on page 95.

Unit 32

2 f, d, e, b, a, c

4 *Suggested answers*
1 I think it failed because they had cashflow problems.
2 It could be because it was the right product at the right time.
3 Maybe she asked the boss at a good time / the business was doing well.
4 Perhaps he just didn't fit in there.

5 *Suggested answers*
1 Well done! / Congratulations!
2 Oh dear, I'm sorry to hear that. Better luck next time.
3 Oh dear. What went wrong?
4 Great!

Pronunciation 2
/s/ slow, some, soon, supermarket, this
/z/ chains, congratulations, result, these

Answer key

Unit 33

4 1 d 2 c 3 a 4 b

5 Shall we start?
The reason we're here today is to decide on …
Does everybody have a copy of the agenda?
Let's start with …
Let's look at the next point now.
Let's move on to …

Pronunciation 1
1 down 2 up

Pronunciation 2
1 ↗ 2 ↗ 3 ↗ 4 ↘ 5 ↗ 6 ↘ 7 ↘

Unit 34

2 The City Star

3 1 10kg 2 carbon fibre 3 40cm 4 4 seconds 5 $850

Pronunciation 1
There are 14.
1 The City Star's lighter than the Lux.
2 It's better than the bigger one.
3 This film's older than that one.
4 The size is the same as the blue bike.

Unit 35

2 1 green 2 blue 3 red 4 yellow

3 *Suggested answer*
The holiday rental market has boomed for various reasons. One is that it seems to offer better value for money than traditional hotels. Also, new communication technology and the rise of the sharing economy have encouraged consumers to make more personalised choices of accommodation.

Pronunciation 1
1 /d/ 2 /d/ 3 /t/ 4 /d/ 5 /t/ 6 /t/

4 *Suggested answers*
1 only a few people
2 most people
3 over half
4 doubled
5 increased their market share
6 is expanding

5 *Suggested answers*
1 It has grown every year.
2 They will probably grow rapidly after 2022.
3 It has expanded dramatically.

6 1 grow strongly 2 compared to 3 fall slightly 4 due to
5 market leader 6 overtake

Unit 36

3 1 communicate with employees 2 check in
3 communication across departments 4 e-mails
5 connected to (their) work 6 apps
7 Check information 8 waste time and money
9 remotely 10 (really) safe

4 1 b 2 c 3 a

Unit 37

1 1 e 2 h 3 i 4 f 5 b 6 a 7 c 8 j 9 d 10 g

Pronunciation 1
1 Ja<u>pan</u>   Japa<u>nese</u>
2 <u>It</u>aly   I<u>tal</u>ian
3 <u>Chi</u>na   Chi<u>nese</u>
4 Viet<u>nam</u>   Vietna<u>mese</u>
5 <u>Eu</u>rope   Euro<u>pe</u>an
6 <u>E</u>gypt   E<u>gyp</u>tian

4 2 How many euros are there?
There are a few (euros).
3 How much plastic is there?
There's a lot (of plastic).
4 How much water is there?
There's a little (water).
5 How many diamonds are there?
There are a few (diamonds).
6 How much oil is there?
There's a lot (of oil).
7 How much money is there?
There's a lot (of money).
8 How much rice is there?
There's a little (rice).
9 How much silver is there?
There's a lot (of silver).
10 How much time is there?
There's a little (time).

Unit 38

1 To many cultures, it looks disrespectful to greet a senior person like a president with your hand in your pocket.

2 *Suggested answers*
1 In Japan, it's better to follow the lead of your hosts. They may either bow or shake hands.
2 Make sure you learn some basic information about a place before you visit.
3 In some Islamic cultures, it's polite for visitors to cover their arms, shoulders and knees in public.
4 In many cultures (including the UK), it's considered rude to be late for appointments.
5 Different cultures have different ideas about what is comfortable in terms of personal space.
6 As a dinner guest in Germany, you shouldn't sit at the table until you are invited.
7 In some Asian cultures, if you finish everything on your plate, it's a sign that your host hasn't given you enough to eat.
8 The exchange of business cards is very important in Japanese culture. You should accept cards with respect and study them.
9 In some cultures, messages are communicated less directly than in others.
10 In the early stages of getting to know someone, it may be unusual to ask personal questions, including those relating to income.
11 Asking for a bag to take away uneaten food is normal in the US (and increasingly so in other countries).
12 Giving an even number of flowers is not welcomed in Russia, except at funerals.
13 The response to the introduction is considered too informal by the host.
14 Hand gestures can mean different things in different cultures.
15 Touching people on the back or head is considered insulting in some cultures.

Unit 39

2 Generally positive

3 1 agricultural 2 machinery 3 2 million 4 growing
5 4.5% 6 higher

4 1 agricultural sector 2 currency 3 industrial sector
4 inflation 5 manufacturing sector 6 property prices
7 public spending 8 unemployment 9 energy/renewables

5 1 f 2 b 3 d 4 i 5 c 6 a 7 h 8 e 9 g

Pronunciation 1
1 ec<u>o</u>nomy   econ<u>o</u>mics   econ<u>o</u>mical
2 <u>in</u>dustry   in<u>dus</u>trial
3 <u>ag</u>riculture   agri<u>cul</u>tural
4 <u>man</u>ufacture   manu<u>fac</u>turing

Teacher's feedback sheet

Name: .... Date: ....

Use this page to monitor students' speaking performances and provide them with feedback.

Grammar	Vocabulary	Functions and expressions	Pronunciations

Picture credits:
4.1 Shutterstock (George Rudy), New York; 4.2 Shutterstock (Gorodenkoff), New York; 4.3 Shutterstock (Syda Productions), New York; 4.4 Shutterstock (Golubovy), New York; 4.5 Shutterstock (Roman Samborskyi), New York; 4.6 Shutterstock (nd3000), New York; 6.1 Shutterstock (VLADGRIN), New York; 6.2 Shutterstock (El Nariz), New York; 8.1 Getty Images (Hill Street Studios), München; 8.2 Getty Images (PeopleImages), München; 10.1 Getty Images (Dave_Pot), München; 11.1 Getty Images (jacklooser), München; 12.1 Getty Images (skynesher), München; 14.1 Getty Images (PeterSnow), München; 16.1 Getty Images (7immy), München; 17.1 Getty Images (PRImageFactory), München; 26/27.1 Shutterstock (Galyna_P), New York; 17.1 © Red Bull Deutschland GmbH; 18.2 Getty Images (PandaVector), München; 20.1 Getty Images (Klaus Vedfelt), München; 22.1 Shutterstock (Monkey Business Images), New York; 23.1 Getty Images (Steve Debenport), München; 27.1 Shutterstock (Volosina), New York; 27.2 Shutterstock (andersphoto), New York; 27.3 Shutterstock (Nattika), New York; 27.4 Shutterstock (Elovich), New York; 27.5 Shutterstock (Jaroslaw Grudzinski), New York; 27.6 Shutterstock (Peter Zijlstra), New York; 27.7 Shutterstock (Africa Studio), New York; 27.8 Shutterstock (Nattika), New York; 27.9 Shutterstock (Aprilphoto), New York; 27.10 Shutterstock (Elovich), New York; 27.11 Shutterstock (irin-k), New York; 27.12 Shutterstock (Africa Studio), New York; 29 Getty Images (DrAfter123), München; 31.2 Shutterstock (sungong), New York; 31.3 Shutterstock (Dim Tik), New York; 31.4 Shutterstock (Neokryuger), New York; 31.5 Shutterstock (intararit), New York; 33.1 Shutterstock (MJTH), New York; 34 Shutterstock (joachim affeldt), New York; mit freundlicher Genehmigung von Unilever; 34 Shutterstock (ricochet64), New York; mit freundlicher Genehmigung der Allianz Deutschland AG; 34.2 Shutterstock (Jonathan Weiss), New York; mit freundlicher Genehmigung von BP Europa SE; 34.5 Inter IKEA Systems B.V.; 36.1 Getty Images (Mel Svenson), München; 36.2 Getty Images (terra24), München; 36.3 Getty Images (Mark-W-R), München; 36.4 Getty Images (simonkr), München; 36.6 Getty Images (guenterguni), München; 36.6 Getty Images (shapecharge), München; 37.1 Getty Images (atakss), München; 37.2 Getty Images (Creative Crop), München; 37.3 Getty Images (Udomsook), München; 37.4 Getty Images (jallfree), München; 37.5 Getty Images (Pogotskiy), München; 37.6 Getty Images (TKphotography64), München; 38.1 Oticon; 40.1 Getty Images (Wenjie Dong), München; 42.1 Getty Images (andrewgenn), München; 44.1 Getty Images (KatBuslaeva), München; 45.1 Getty Images (Siberian Photographer), München; 48.1 Getty Images (Jupiterimages), München; 49.1 Getty Images (andresr), München; 50.1 Shutterstock (Monkey Business Images), New York; 52.1 Getty Images (kgfoto), München; 52.2 Shutterstock (Guan jiangchi), New York; 52.3 Shutterstock (Olga Popova), New York; 54.3 Getty Images (andresr), München; 54.4 Getty Images (stockstudioX), München; 54.5 Getty Images (Andrew Olney), München; 54.6 Getty Images (Willowpix), München; 56.1 Getty Images (Bhavesh1988), München; 58.1 Getty Images (Johnny Greig), München; 60.1 Getty Images (Yayasya), München; 61.1 Shutterstock (Leah-Anne Thompson), New York; 62.1 Shutterstock (imassimo82), New York; 63.1 Getty Images (Grafissimo), München; 63.2 Getty Images (Art Wager), München; 63.3 Shutterstock (Erik Tanghe), New York; 63.4 Getty Images (CarmenMurillo), München; 63.5 Getty Images (sturti), München; 63.6 Getty Images (pluem05), München; 67.1 Shutterstock (marekuliasz), New York; 70.1 Getty Images (Eshma), München; 70.2 Getty Images (Winai_Tepsuttinun), München; 70.3 Getty Images (anurakpong), München; 75.1 Shutterstock (Alexey Boldin), New York; 75.2 Shutterstock (Oleksiy Mark), New York; 75.3 Shutterstock (Oleksiy Mark), New York; 76.1 Shutterstock (Travel mania), New York; 77.1 Getty Images (HAYKIRDI), München; 77.2 Getty Images (gaffera), München; 77.3 Shutterstock (photka), New York; 77.4 Shutterstock (bankbee), New York; 77.5 Getty Images (polarica), München; 77.6 Getty Images (The-Tor), München; 77.7 Getty Images (mgkaya), München; 77.8 Shutterstock (Africa Studio), New York; 77.9 Getty Images (CapturedByAmelia), München; 77.10 Getty Images (jamesteohart), München; 78.1 picture-alliance (Yonhap), Frankfurt; 80.1 Getty Images (Slavica), München; 80.2 Getty Images (AlpamayoPhoto), München; 80.3 Getty Images (PhotoBylove), München; 80.4 Getty Images (4khz), München; 80.5 Getty Images (Monty Rakusen), München; 80.6 Getty Images (moodboard), München; 80.7 Shutterstock (Syda Productions), New York; 80.8 Getty Images (annestahl), München; 80.9 Shutterstock (imacoconut), New York; 82.1 Shutterstock (kojala), New York; 82.2 Shutterstock (admin_design), New York; 82.3 Shutterstock (Kathy Hutchins), New York; 83.1 Shutterstock (Exclusive Dn), New York; 83.2 Shutterstock (Yasonya), New York; 83.3 Getty Images, München; 83.4 Shutterstock (claudio zaccherini), New York; 83.5 Shutterstock (trekandshoot), New York; 85.1 Shutterstock (PixieMe), New York; 86.1 Shutterstock (Larisa Blinova), New York; **Cover** Shutterstock (Rawpixel.com), New York; **online** Shutterstock (MilanMarkovic78), New York; **online** Shutterstock (TaTum2003), New York

Illustration credits:
Beehive Illustration: Mike Philips (66), Vince Reid (24, 68), Rory Walker (64, 65, 78, 79), Nigel Dobbyn (31.1) Oxford Designers and Illustrators Ltd: (60, 61, 86)